Healer's Guide to Plants & Herbs for Anxiety

Herbal Remedies for Mental Health

Lydia Odenat, PhD

DANTOR PRESS

Copyright © [2024] by Lydia Odenat

Author's Note:

This book is sold to readers with the understanding that while the author aims to inform, enlighten, and provide accurate general information regarding the subject matter covered, the author is not engaged in providing medical or other professional advice or assistance. The information in this book is intended only as an informative guide for those wishing to learn and understand mental health issues. This book is not intended to replace or conflict with the advice offered by a medical professional.

DANTOR PRESS: 1640 Powers Ferry Rd., 20-200, Marietta GA 30067

Printed in the United States of America. First Edition: June 2024

Published by Dantor Press

ISBN: 979-8-9882999-3-6 (hardback)

ISBN: 979-8-9882999-0-5 (paperback)

ISBN: 979-8-9882999-1-2 (ebook)

Contents

Part One

Herbal Medicine

Chapter 1

History of Medicinal Herbs

Since time immemorial, indigenous people have sought communion with the botanical world around them. Ancient wisdom, carried forth from generation to generation, allowed our ancestors to understand and utilize the innumerable healing properties of their natural landscapes. From dormant seed to inner bark, through creeping rhizomes and fibrous roots, our people vigilantly studied the bountiful gifts of plant life. Ancient herbalists prescribed these plants, in part or whole, to treat illnesses and conditions that ailed everyday people. This is where the art *and* science of herbology were born.

How did we come to know so much about the healing properties of plants and herbs? Ancient healers acquired herbal knowledge through a vast array of channels. Some communed intimately with their spiritual ancestors, turning their eyes *upward* and utilizing sacred rituals to translate plant language into human understanding. Others turned their attention *inward* and relied heavily on intuition to access an eternal well of herbal knowledge. Yet and still, others turned their gaze *outward* to the physical world, venturing deeply into the wild to barter directly with the wetlands, woodlands, and grasslands. These healers utilized their natural senses to take inventory of the plants they encountered. Communing with nature in this manner involved using their bodies as the primary instruments of inquiry. Through meticulous observation and sampling, they used their sense of smell, touch, taste, sight, sound, and interoception to explore the gifts that each plant came to bear.

Other ancient healers were led to their discoveries through an ability to keenly and astutely observe the behaviors of animals in their natural habitats. As curious spectators, these early scientists noted when the lemur nibbled on tamarind or when the bonobo ingested Manniophyton fulvum to treat intestinal parasites. This method gave way to zoopharmacognosy, an entire field of study devoted to exploring how animals self-medicate in nature. Through trial and error, whether experiential or spiritual, these collective acts required a total immersion in the world of plants. These varied *methods of knowing* gave way to a wealth of information, transferred from animal to people, spirit to people, plant to people, and people to people, refined over time into a collective repository of medicinal knowledge. As once asserted by the world-renowned ethnobotanist Dr. Anthony Kweku Andoh, the plants *themselves* desired to be known and valuable to man.

Herbal healers have been known by many names. Leaf doctors, medicine wo/men, elders, midwives, priests, priestesses, mambos, shamans, houngans, and mystics were among the countless titles they carried. Regardless of the appellation, they each served a vital role in ensuring their people's spiritual, physical, communal, and psychoemotional health and wellness. Through years (and generations) of dedicated learning, these women and men engaged in highly valued practices in their communities. The seeds, roots, bark, leaves, berries, and flowers administered in teas, tinctures, salves, extracts, and baths helped promote healing and relief from everyday suffering.

Today, we are witnessing a burgeoning desire to *return* to this ancient practice of phytomedicine. The old ways of knowing and communing with plant life resurface due to a growing desire (perhaps need) to reconnect with land and soil. As we all know, the tradition of herbal medicine never entirely disappeared but has taken an undeserved back seat to orthodox medical practices. But the tides of change are upon us, and modern people increasingly long for simpler and intuitive healing practices. We all desire healing systems that are not entirely governed by the "medical industrial complex" of insurance companies, pharmaceutical corporations, the U.S. Food and Drug Administration (FDA), professional medical associations, and the lobbyists who represent them. Many are taking notice that our society, as a whole, is becoming sicker, experiencing a poorer quality of life, and witnessing shorter life expectancies (even though our children, adults, and pets are more medicated than ever before). Many are seeking an alternative. A path that reconnects our lives to the natural fruits of our planet.

Despite the changing tides, there is no denying that advancements in modern medicine, with all its technologies, tools, and devices, have improved our overall quality of life. This book does not call for a moratorium on the use of psychotropic medication in the treatment of mental health disorders. Instead, the goal is to present an alternative option that compels readers to explore natural remedies as one of many paths to addressing mental health problems and concerns. In other words, there is no replacing modern medicine as we know it. However, there remains ample room and opportunity for people to utilize herbs to manage mental health symptoms, aid in recovery from emotional stressors and injury, and achieve optimal states of psycho-socioemotional wellness in the face of challenging times.

This shift requires that we reject the notion that nature is our enemy. We must learn to embrace the life forms growing along our driveways, backyards, and the wooded lots surrounding our communities. Once we overcome our fear of the natural world, we will discover there is medicine there.

Chapter 2

What is an Herb?

W hen it comes to herbal medicine, the term 'herb' is often used. But what exactly is an herb? The word 'herb' is derived from the Latin word 'herba', which means 'grassy or green plant'. In the context of herbal medicine, 'herb' is often used to refer to any non-woody plant that is valued for its medicinal, culinary, cosmetic, or aromatic properties. In this guide, we will use the terms 'herb' and 'plant' interchangeably. This means that when we say 'herb', we could also be referring to medicinal trees, shrubs, and grasses.

As noted in the introductory chapter, herbs play a significant and integral role in the lives of humans and animals and in the maintenance of our entire ecosystem. Botanical medicine or herbalism (the study or practice of using plants as medicine) has existed in every civilization, among all groups of people, and in every region of the world. The book aims to honor and respect those time-tested herbal traditions found among varying groups of people around the globe, emphasizing the importance of preserving and valuing our shared cultural heritage.

Herbalism is closely intertwined with many cultural and

spiritual practices worldwide. For many traditions, the entire community plays an active role in an individual's healing process. Through this collectivist worldview, the medicinal herb alone (without the cultural or community context) renders it useless and insufficient. For this matter, readers are encouraged to inquire into the intersections of their identities with the spiritual and cultural histories of the plants they use or recommend to others. It is important to investigate the rich traditions that helped shape our understanding of each herb, as well as honor the land from where the herbs take root. This guide only provides readers with a basic overview of each plant's traditional uses, physical attributes, applications to mental health, and relevant research on therapeutic efficacy.

Accessing Herbal Medicine

Acquiring the herbs outlined in this book will require patience, intentionality, and unwavering diligence. Select high-quality, organically grown, and ethically sourced plant material whenever possible to achieve optimal results. Purchasing quality herbs at international food markets or health food stores may be most accessible for people living in or near metropolitan areas with large immigrant populations. This is especially true for markets specializing in Asian, African, Caribbean, or Native American goods. In major cities with large Asian communities, seek out shops specializing in Ayurvedic or Traditional Chinese Medicine. Readers should not overlook urban gardens, farmer's markets, local nurseries, and other resources in the community.

For those in rural and remote communities, sleepy coastal towns, or mountainous regions, the opportunity to forage the wild for medicinal plants native to their environment can be a truly rewarding experience. It is a chance to connect with nature and discover the abundance of healing plants that surround them. Many of the herbs listed in this book may be growing in abundance right in their backyards. To uncover these hidden treasures, a comprehensive survey of the land is necessary, along with an inventory of what grows naturally. Smartphone apps (ex: Picture This) can be a valuable tool, allowing users to photograph and identify plants quickly and efficiently.

When it comes to shopping for herbs, it is crucial to have a clear understanding of which plant parts are required for herbal remedies. Some plants only contain medicinal properties in their leaves, while others are concentrated in the root. Some remedies utilize only plant seeds because the rest of the plant contains toxic chemical compounds. Therefore, it is essential for readers to take note of the parts traditionally used for each plant, every time they prepare a remedy. This knowledge is the key to unlocking the full potential of the herbs.

Harvesting plant material at the right time of year in the plant's development is also critical. The best harvest time for flowers is around peak bloom, for leaves and other aerial parts in the late morning, and for roots when the plant is fully mature and dormant in the Fall. For seeds, only harvest when the plant fully matures (just before seeds fall). After harvesting, one must decide which herbal preparations are most suitable for administration. Remedies may be administered in cold or hot infusions, decoctions, concoctions, tinctures, extracts, essential oils, capsules, salves, poultices, and baths (see glossary for definitions of each term). The method that allows a plant to retain its maximum medicinal benefits should be prioritized.

When foraging for a particular plant, take only what is needed, which is a practice that helps conserve and protect the plant's future. Not doing so may lead to over-harvesting and extinction of plant species over time. As a general rule, harvesting should be limited to 10%-15% of any given plant in any given area. One must also seek to protect the plant's integrity by minimizing disturbances to its natural state. An example is harvesting plant bark by only taking from lateral branches (not the main trunk). This will ensure that the plant thrives and will be available to future generations. And above all, I recommend that exceptionally rare plants *be left alone.* When uncertain, remember to consult your local botanical organizations. They are there to guide and support you in identifying threatened and endangered plant species.

For those unable to access or acquire plants in their local environments, the following options exist:

1. Order tinctures, extracts, elixirs, oils, or dried bulk herbs from online platforms. Online stores worth trying include Sacred Vibes Apothecary, Mountain Rose Herbs, Frontier Co-op, Anima Mundi Apothecary, Starwest Botanicals, Frontier Co-op, Faire, Veladya Organica, Xálish Medicines, Herb Pharm, Herbalist and Alchemist.

2. Order seeds online and start an herb garden. If ordering exotic plants from other regions or countries, check with local organizations/agencies to ensure that the plant will not be problematic or disruptive to the local ecosystem.

3. Seek out local farmers and herbalists. They are key resources for learning and acquiring specific herbs, fostering community engagement, and supporting local businesses.

4. Connect with local herbalism groups and organizations where plants and seeds may be swapped or bartered.

5. Visit local nurseries to see what herbs are carried and inquire about their ability to order and supply herbs in bulk.

A critical element in herbal medicine is learning to properly acquire, handle, store, dose, and administer medicinal plants. In addition to space, herbalism requires specific supplies and tools for proper administration. The goal is to create a temperature and light controlled space where plants and herbs can optimally grow and thrive. Recommended items include:

1 Shelving units or cabinets
2 Glass jars or containers
3 Mixing bowls
4 Mortal and pestle
5 Labels and markers
6 Cleaning supplies
7 Packing materials
8 Dropper bottles

Chapter 3

Anxiety Management

According to the World Health Organization, 301 million people worldwide suffer from an anxiety disorder[29]. Prevalence studies also indicate that approximately 10% of people in "Western countries" suffer from anxiety (rates are consistently lower in the Global South). Anxiety remains the most commonly reported mental health concern among people seeking psychiatric services. When left untreated, symptoms tend to worsen over time, with very few people recovering without some form of intervention. Despite these findings, only 1 out of 4 people receive treatment for their symptoms[29].

As defined by the current Diagnostic Statistical Manual of Mental Disorders (DSM-5)[39], a generalized anxiety disorder is characterized by chronic worry and excessive anxious mood surrounding several events and situations in a person's life. The worrisome thoughts and anxious mood remain persistent, uncontrollable, and disproportionate to the actual likelihood or impact of the feared event or situation. In addition, these symptoms must interfere with the person's daily functioning and impact their ability to relax, concentrate, sleep, manage reactivity to stressors, or maintain normal energy levels.

When split into the mind-body continuum, anxiety is best understood by examining the various systems it impairs (i.e., mind, emotional, physical, and social). The "mind symptoms" often include persistent worry, cognitive vigilance, psychological tension, anxious thoughts, preoccupation with thoughts, and problems with attention, concentration, and encoding memory. The "emotional symptoms" include irritability, fear, nervousness, distress, agitation, and emotional numbing or exhaustion. The most commonly reported "body symptoms" include muscle and motor tension, fatigue, shortness of breath, chest pressure, heart palpitations, hypersensitivity to stimulation, psychomotor agitation, restlessness, tension headaches, gastrointestinal problems, urinary urgency, tremors, shaking, sleep problems, dizziness, unsteadiness, feeling excessively hot, and other symptoms associated with autonomic hyperactivity. For the most chronic sufferers of anxiety, the "social symptoms" include withdrawal, isolation, hypervigilance, situational detachment, and an inability to be mindfully present while engaging with others (see figure 1 A).

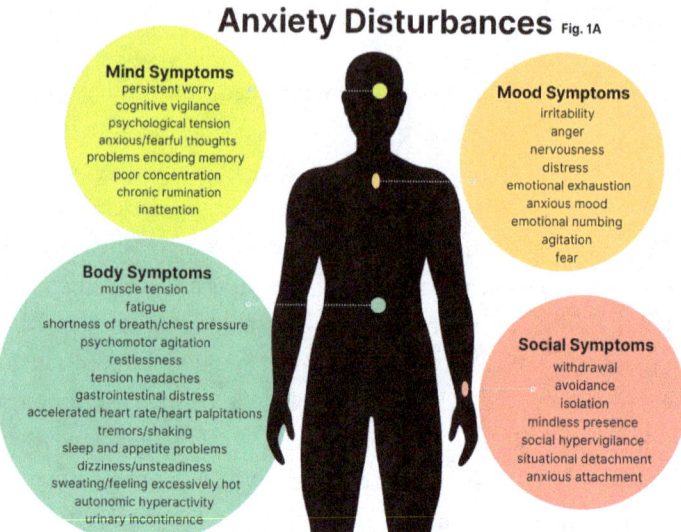

Anxiety Disturbances Fig. 1A

Mind Symptoms
persistent worry
cognitive vigilance
psychological tension
anxious/fearful thoughts
problems encoding memory
poor concentration
chronic rumination
inattention

Mood Symptoms
irritability
anger
nervousness
distress
emotional exhaustion
anxious mood
emotional numbing
agitation
fear

Body Symptoms
muscle tension
fatigue
shortness of breath/chest pressure
psychomotor agitation
restlessness
tension headaches
gastrointestinal distress
accelerated heart rate/heart palpitations
tremors/shaking
sleep and appetite problems
dizziness/unsteadiness
sweating/feeling excessively hot
autonomic hyperactivity
urinary incontinence

Social Symptoms
withdrawal
avoidance
isolation
mindless presence
social hypervigilance
situational detachment
anxious attachment

Fig. 1A

There are a number of empirically supported psychotherapy interventions for anxiety disorders. Among them, cognitive behavioral therapy (CBT) is extolled as the most effective and well-researched form of treatment. This therapeutic approach emphasizes the role of thought processes (cognitions) in the manifestation of emotions and behaviors. The basic tenet of CBT is that negative emotions and problematic behaviors are anchored in "maladaptive" thought processes, interpretations, and assumptions. CBT aims to help people identify and revise these thought processes and replace them with alternative cognitions and behaviors that foster healthier responses. Other evidence-based anxiety interventions applied to anxiety include psychodynamic therapy, acceptance and commitment therapy (ACT), dialectical behavioral therapy (DBT), and different variations of CBT (i.e., exposure and mindfulness-based cognitive therapies). A newer and emerging form of treatment called somatic therapy is also showing promise in its ability to treat anxiety. Somatic therapy focuses less on cognitions and more on engaging the bodily manifestations of symptoms.

As a psychologist, I have found that the most effective treatments for anxiety are multi-pronged, integrative, and tailored to meet the individual needs of clients. The treatment may include elements of cognitive-behavioral and somatic therapy interventions, adoption of mindfulness-based and relaxation practices, healthy lifestyle changes (e.g., diet, exercise, and sleep), utilization of social and community/cultural supports, psychiatric medications, and wellness-oriented interventions (i.e., massage therapy, fitness, acupuncture, biofeedback, energy work). Any approach to treating anxiety should include an investigation of possible underlying medical conditions, namely, hyperthyroidism, adrenal dysfunction, or undiagnosed heart conditions. These conditions often manifest in the form of anxiety and must be addressed as the root cause. Healers who work with anxious sufferers ought to thoroughly assess each person's history and collaborate with any professional (i.e., primary care providers, nutritionists, psychiatrists, clinical herbalists) involved in their care. The assessment should include a full exploration of problematic cultural beliefs, values, attitudes, and ideologies that may exacerbate symptoms.

Healers who utilize this book must take a holistic approach to understanding mental health and wellness. They must adopt a contextual lens that examines the role of biological/genetic vulnerabilities, environmental stressors and toxins, lifestyle patterns (i.e., sleep, diet, exercise), and the socioeconomic and political factors involved in disease etiology and progression. The contextualization of wellness consists of exploring cultural identity, practices, and beliefs and the role of generational legacies in overall health status. Another equally important requirement is the awareness that the body is an instrument that must be nurtured and maintained at all levels. This instrument demands quality food, healthy relationships, and balanced environments for daily sustenance. It is counterintuitive to administer herbs to manage anxiety while consistently exposing the body to emotional and environmental assault.

This book is for *all healers*, including mental health professionals, clinical herbalists, nutritionists, nurses, physicians, chiropractors, massage therapists, and other wellness-oriented providers. Its goal is to provide an easy-to-use resource to share with anxious sufferers, particularly those whose anxiety hinders their ability to function optimally in their daily lives. It is important to note that this book is not a demand but *an invitation* to a more natural approach to wellness. It invites individuals to explore herbal medicine as *one of many* viable options on their healing journey. Respect for individual and personal autonomy is paramount and no one should ever feel pressured to utilize plant medicine. And at no point should an individual discontinue their medical regimen without consulting a treating provider.

This book is also for readers who are seeking to improve their mental health and well-being. The herbs listed within these pages have the potential to alleviate suffering and lift the heavy veil of anxiety. These plants and herbs were selected for their ability to treat and manage a range of emotional, cognitive, and physical symptoms. May this book offer a respite from suffering, whether in the form of a leaf tea or bark tincture that helps manage day-to-day reactivity to triggers, ease bodily tension, or slow things down enough to draw upon one's own coping resources.

Chapter 4

Cautionary Note

People who incorporate holistic and herbal medicine into their daily regimen must always consult with a primary care provider (or specialist) before embarking on this journey. This is especially important for those diagnosed with chronic illnesses and prescribed medication. Despite being "natural," herbal remedies can elicit adverse reactions and severe side effects when taken alone or combined with conventional medication. Not all plants are safe, and many must be handled with the utmost caution. Collaborative care with a physician, psychotherapist, naturopath, or trained clinical herbalist may be essential to ensuring safety and well-being.

The effective use of this guide requires absolute precaution in the handling, storing, dosing, and administering of every herb (even the "safe" ones). For healers, this involves an absolute commitment to constant monitoring and evaluation of symptoms and outcomes. This can be accomplished by performing periodic assessments using inventories, surveys, symptom logs, psychological tests, and medical instruments.

For those who are not "healers" but utilize this book to manage their symptoms, periodic assessments remain necessary. Assessments may take the form of mood journals or other systematic methods of logging daily symptom changes.

When determining whether one is an appropriate fit for the herbs listed in this guide, the following must be assessed:

- Risk of suicidal behavior or history of engaging in self-harm or self-injurious behaviors
- Cultural and personal beliefs that serve as barriers to optimal mental health
- Current health status and medical history (especially medically-complex histories) that require consultation with a primary care provider
- Willingness to integrate other complementary approaches and lifestyle changes into treatment (i.e., diet, exercise, sleep, abstinence from drugs/alcohol, talk therapy, mindfulness practices, social support)
- Vulnerability to substance abuse, addiction, or chemical dependence
- Exposure to ongoing/chronic environmental stressors and toxins
- Progression of symptoms
- History of sensitivity to herbal remedies and supplements
- History of treatment resistance to other interventions, including psychotropic medications
- The severity of psychological symptoms and level of impairment (acute and debilitating symptoms may be better suited for psychotropic and other interventions before trying herbal remedies)

- Access to healthcare resources (in the event symptoms worsen)
- Access to adequate community and social supports during the acute phase of symptoms

Part Two

Plants & Herbs for Anxiety

American Ginseng

K nown by the botanical name Panax quinquefolius, this slow-growing perennial grows in the rich woods of the American Midwest and Eastern states. It can be recognized by its bright red kidney-shaped berries, sharp-toothed oval leaflets, tiny flowers, and gnarled roots. As of today, ninety-seven percent of American Ginseng is grown in Wisconsin[87] [96] and it is widely used as an ingredient in beverages.

Historical/Traditional Uses: American ginseng remains widely celebrated for its adaptogenic and restorative qualities. A member of the Araliaceae (Ginseng) family, it has long been used to promote concentration, improve mental efficiency, and reduce nervous tension. Research studies suggest that American ginseng significantly improves sleep quality, mood, and energy levels in adults who consume a standardized extract over four months[15]. Much like ginseng trees, which are said to live up to a thousand years, herbalists firmly believe in American ginseng's ability to promote longevity, vitality, resilience, and stamina[3].

Psychobotanical Uses: American ginseng is ideal for anxiety sufferers who report nervous agitation[14] and chronic fatigue[3], coupled with deficits in attention, concentration, and memory[3][15]. Eclectic physicians of the 19th century touted its ability to treat mental exhaustion, anxiety-related digestive problems, and "nervous debility"[84]. As an adaptogen, American ginseng helps improve one's ability to emotionally cope with mental stressors and recover from cognitive fatigue[14][96]. Taking over three months may also improve the body's ability to regulate stress hormones[3].

Guidance: The root of American ginseng is the primary part used medicinally. For decoctions, 3-6 grams of dried whole root may be steeped in 1 cup of boiling water for 25-30 minutes. Let cool for ten minutes before consuming. Drink one cup daily (preferably in the morning) for 2-3 weeks. Discontinue use for 14 days, then resume daily use for another 2-3 weeks. Continue this cycle for at least three months. For tincture, add 1 part dried root to 4 parts 30% alcohol (may substitute with vegetable glycerin or apple cider vinegar). Take 3 to 7 drops, 1-3 times daily. If using a commercial extract, follow the instructions on the package. Adverse effects may include insomnia.

Asafoetida

N ative to Northern Africa, the Middle East, and Central Asia, this gum resin from the tall perennial ferula plant is a commonly used spice and flavoring agent (e.g, the distinct flavor in Worcestershire sauce). Known botanically as Ferula asafoetida, this pungent and aromatic plant belongs to the Apiaceae family (Carrot and Parsley family). It is recognized by its bushy clusters of bright yellow flowers that attract many types of pollinators.

Historical/Traditional Uses: Asafoetida's resin is derived from the plant's roots/rhizomes and has long been used in African American folk herbalism and Ayurvedic medicine as a digestive aid, expectorant, aphrodisiac, laxative, and sedative[40][45][103]. Early records document its used among enslaved Africans who "wore it around their necks to ward off illness and promote health."[103] Traditional herbalists support its application in managing irritable bowel syndrome, asthma, hypertension, insect bites, diabetes, digestive problems, and improving brain health[45][96].

Psychobotanical Uses: A lesser-known fact is Asafoetida's use as a remedy for nervous disorders. It was commonly prescribed throughout the 19th century for the treatment of "hysteria," mood swings, and depression[3]. Eclectic physicians of this time lauded its ability to treat "nervous depression," "nervous irritation," and anxiety-induced headaches[84]. It also helps manage muscle spasms, stimulate the central nervous system, and resolve digestive problems associated with anxiety.

Guidance: Asafoetida is primarily found in powder form. It may be consumed as a warm beverage or taken in capsule form. For beverages, add 1 gram of Asafoetida powder to 1 cup of warm water. Stir and drink one cup daily. For capsules, take 250 mg daily. Avoid during pregnancy and while taking blood thinners.

Ashwagandha

This evergreen shrub grows in the drier regions of India, Pakistan, West Africa, South Africa, and the Middle East. It is commonly known as Indian Ginseng, Poison gooseberry, and Winter cherry and belongs to the Solanaceae family (i.e., the Nightshades). Known scientifically as Withania somnifera, Ashwagandha has been successfully cultivated in the southern areas of the United States (primarily hardiness zones 7a and higher). Its leaves are collected in the spring, and the roots are dug up in the Fall[16].

Traditional/Historical Uses: West African folk healers utilized freshly pounded Ashwagandha to treat fevers, chills, and rheumatism, while the Swazi of South Africa used it for smallpox[59]. Traditional Ayurvedic practitioners revered Ashwagandha for more than 3,000 years, and celebrated this plant for its adaptogenic qualities. It was valued for its ability to improve vitality, promote rejuvenation, and improve recovery from illness[3][11][96]. Ashwagandha has also been used in folk medicine to treat arthritis, inflammation, low libido, muscle pain, hyperthyroidism, fibromyalgia, infertility, hypertension, and age-related cognitive decline[3][11][15].

Psychobotanical Uses: Ashwagandha helps ease the body back into the here-and-now, promoting a sense of grounding. Research studies on the effects of Ashwagandha have shown significant reductions in anxiety and stress levels among adult patients, with few noted side effects[11][15]. Ashwagandha has long been recognized as an effective nervine with significant mood-stabilizing effects. It promotes relaxation, reduces stress, mitigates mental exhaustion, minimizes anxious mood, decreases insomnia, and ameliorates stress-related sexual problems[3][15][16][43]. It eases tension, reduces "mental chatter"[3], improves concentration, reduces cognitive fogginess, promotes calm sleep, and strengthens mental performance. Recent clinical trials have demonstrated that Ashwagandha (paired with dietary changes) may be more effective at reducing anxiety than psychotherapy alone[8][11]. Animal studies have also demonstrated that Ashwagandha induces anxiolytic effects comparable to lorazepam[66]. It is also helpful in managing restless leg syndrome[96].

Guidance: The whole Ashwagandha plant (i.e., root, leaves, flowers, and berries) may be used medicinally. Consume fresh or dried plant material in tea or tincture form. For tea, steep 1 tsp of dried plant material in 1 cup of freshly boiling water for 15-30 minutes. If using in powder form, add 2 tsp of root powder to 1 cup of water or milk. Stir and consume. Honey may be added for flavor enhancement. For tincture, add 1 part plant material to 5 parts 70% alcohol (may substitute with vegetable glycerin or apple cider vinegar). Consume 1-2 tsp three times daily. If using a commercial product, follow the instructions on the package. Must consult a primary care doctor before use. This is especially necessary if diagnosed with hypertension, diabetes, thyroid, or autoimmune disorders. Avoid during pregnancy. It is not recommended while taking medication for anxiety, sleep, or seizure disorders[3].

Bacopa

This small, creeping perennial plant has been utilized for centuries by Ayurvedic doctors in India. It goes by many names, including Herb-of-grace, Indian pennywort, water hyssop, and Brahmi ("holy," "divine," and "devout"). Bacopa is recognized by its white and purple flowers, and small, oblong and crinkled leaves that can be seen floating in the waters of Florida, Central America, and India[3]. Known by the scientific name Bacopa monnieri, this hardy and succulent plant belongs to the Plantain family. It thrives in warmer temperatures and tropical climates, including marshlands and the edges of swamplands.

Historical/Traditional Uses: Bacopa is widely recognized in Ayurvedic medicine as a powerful nervine, brain tonic, and adaptogen that supports general brain health, vitality, and cognitive functioning, including learning and concentration[3][8][15][92]. It has also been used to treat high blood pressure, hyperthyroidism, and inflammation[15].

Psychobotanical Uses: An added benefit of Bacopa is its calming effects on anxiety[8][92], including relief from stress/tension, anxiety-related memory loss, and racing thoughts. Research studies on Bacopa indicate that it significantly decreases anxiety and stress among adults given large doses over two weeks[15]. A similar study showed significant reductions in anxiety symptoms among a group of older adults who took 300 mg over twelve weeks. Bacopa helps induce a sense of calm and peace while managing distractibility[3].

Guidance: Bacopa leaves, or the entire plant, may be consumed in tea form (though many complain of its bitter taste). For tea, add 2-4 tsp of plant material to 1 cup of freshly boiling water. Allow to steep for 20 minutes. Drink up to 3 cups per day. For tincture, add 1 part plant material to 5 parts 50% alcohol (may substitute with vegetable glycerin or apple cider vinegar). Consume 1/2 tsp three times daily. Consult with a primary care doctor before use. Avoid if diagnosed with hyperthyroidism. Pregnant or nursing mothers should avoid use. If using a commercial product, follow the instructions on the package.

Baikal (Chinese) Skullcap

This flowering perennial herb has a longstanding history in Asian herbal medicine. Known as Scutellaria or Chinese skullcap, it is native to the region around Lake Baikal (situated in Russia) and northern China. Baikal skullcap is recognized by its purple single-stemmed blooms with lance-shaped leaves. Botanically named Scutellaria baicalensis, it thrives in open grasslands and the wild at elevations below 2,000 feet. It belongs to the Lamiaceae (Mint) family.

Historical/Traditional Uses: Baikal skullcap has been utilized to treat various conditions, including asthma, allergies, hypertension, HIV/AIDS, hepatitis, atherosclerosis, shingles, fevers, and colds[3]. It also has a longstanding history of treating inflammatory diseases[83].

Psychobotanical Uses: Recent studies have demonstrated Baikal Skullcap's effectiveness in managing anxiety and stress symptoms, including tension headaches. In addition to its anxiolytic properties, lab studies show evidence of its neuroprotective and antidepressant effects[38]. The root is medicinal and considered relatively safe/well-tolerated at low doses. Baikal skullcap is not to be confused with the North American skullcap, Scutellaria lateriflora.

Guidance: The root of Baikal skullcap is the primary part used medicinally. It may be consumed in various forms, including teas, tinctures, capsules, and extracts. For root tea, add 2 tsp of dried root to one cup of hot water. Steep for 20-30 minutes and strain. For tincture, add 1 part root to 5 parts of 55% alcohol (may substitute with vegetable glycerin or apple cider vinegar). Consume 1/2 tsp three times daily. If using a commercial product, follow the instructions on the package.

Basil

K nown commonly as Sweet Basil, this aromatic plant remains highly regarded for its culinary and medicinal value. With over one hundred varieties, it falls under the Lamiaceae (Mint) family and is known botanically as Ocimum basilicum. It is recognized by its shiny, dark green, ovate leaves, small white flowers, square stems, and sweet, solid fragrance.

Historical/Traditional Uses: Medicinally, Basil has been used for centuries in the treatment of a host of health conditions (ranging from digestive problems and insect bites[10] to flatulence, stomach cramps, and headaches[1]). It is a natural antimicrobial, antibacterial, and anti-inflammatory agent[6]. The plant is utilized throughout West Africa as a fever reducer and malaria remedy[59]. There are early accounts of its use as a health tonic among enslaved Africans on American plantations[103].

Psychobotanical Uses: Applied to anxiety, herbalists tout Basil's ability to manage irritability, stress, nervous exhaustion, anxiety-related sleep problems, mental fatigue, melancholy, and anxious mood[1][11]. Eclectic physicians identified Basil as a nervine and employed it in the treatment of "mild nervous disorders"[84]. Laboratory studies of its extract oil have also demonstrated its significant anxiolytic and sedative effects[51][59].

Guidance: Basil leaves, stems, and flowering tops are used medicinally and may be consumed as tea or tincture. Basil is also edible, and fresh plant material may be eaten. For tea, 1 tsp of dried leaves (or 2 tsp of fresh) may be added to one cup of boiling water. Allow it to steep and infuse for 10-15 minutes. Strain and drink as needed. For tincture, add 1 part root to 2 parts 40% alcohol (may substitute with vegetable glycerin or apple cider vinegar). Consume 1/2 tsp two times daily.

Regarding accessibility, Basil leaves can be easily grown in containers on decks, balconies, patios, front stoops, and porches. If using a commercial product, follow the instructions on the package. Avoid while pregnant or nursing.

Black Cohosh

This aromatic perennial herb is native to the Northern Hemisphere and can be found throughout the woodlands of Canada and Maine, down to the wilds of Georgia and Florida. It is distinguished by its tiny white flowers, tightly nestled along a tall, wand-like raceme, and sharply-toothed leaflets. This shade-loving plant also bears sharp, toothy leaves that form three lobes. Known botanically as Actaea racemosa, Black cohosh goes by the names squaw root, bugbane, rattle root, menopausal root, and richweed. It belongs to the Ranunculaceae family of flowering plants.

Historical/Traditional Uses: As with the multitude of names, Black cohosh has a multitude of uses. The Cherokee and Iroquois people of North America extensively relied on this plant to alleviate a host of ailments, ranging from rheumatism and snakebites to women's health issues (i.e., problems with menstruation, lactation, and menopause)[5][14] [17]. The Algonquin people used this herb for gynecological complaints[15], while the Penobscot people used it to treat kidney problems[11]. The Gullah Geechee people (African descendants in the lower Atlantic coast) used it to treat intestinal worms in humans and livestock[82]. The name "cohosh" comes from the Algonquin word for "tough," an attribute that describes the plant's gnarled roots[14].

Psychobotanical Uses: Applied to anxiety, Black cohosh is a highly-regarded relaxant, nervine, and sedative. Nineteenth-century eclectic physicians lauded its ability to treat "nervous irritability" and "nervous excitability" and its "undoubted influence over the nervous system"[84]. It is also helpful in ameliorating stress, tension, mild anxiety, depression, and the emotional changes associated with menopause[3] [14]. Clinical studies show that Black cohosh effectively reduces stress hormones in healthy women who consume 200 mg daily for one week[15]. Randomized clinical trials have also found it effective in alleviating hot flashes[14]. Black cohosh is also helpful in the management of agitation, panic symptoms, and mood changes experienced around the menstrual cycle.

Guidance: The dried root and rhizomes of Black cohosh are used medicinally. It may be consumed as a tea, tincture, extract, or in capsule form. For tea, add 2-3 tsp of dried root to 3 cups of water. Allow to sit for 20-30 minutes and consume up to twice daily. For tincture, add 1 part dried root to 5 parts 80% alcohol (may substitute with vegetable glycerin or apple cider vinegar). Consume 1/4 tsp three times daily. If using a commercial product, follow the instructions on the package. Pregnant women should avoid use since it is known to stimulate uterine contractions.

Black Haw

This deciduous shrub is native to the woodlands of Eastern and Central regions of the United States. Also known as sweet haw, it is recognizable by its large clusters of small, flattened white flowers that bloom from spring to summer. It also bears blue-black berries with glossy, pointy, oval-shaped leaves. Known by the scientific name Viburnum prunifolium, this shrub belongs to the Moschatel family.

Historical/Traditional Uses: Indigenous Americans and folk healers have used Black haw for centuries. There is also evidence that enslaved African Americans utilized it as a purgative and decongestant[103]. Tea from its reddish-brown bark and young twigs was commonly administered to aid with women's reproductive health. It has been touted for its diuretic and sedating effects, as well as its ability to treat women's gynecological complaints (i.e., miscarriage, postpartum spasms, painful menses, and uterine prolapse)[5][9][11][84]. It is often substituted for Cramp bark.

Psychobotanical Uses: As a calming nervine, this herb can treat nervousness and induce relaxation among anxious sufferers. Black haw may be especially helpful for postpartum women experiencing anxiety and physical tension.

Guidance: Black haw is typically consumed as bark tea or tincture. For decoctions, add 1-2 tsp per cup of boiling water and allow to simmer for 15-20 minutes. Strain and drink up to 3 cups per day. For tincture, add 1 part dried bark to 5 parts 50% alcohol (may substitute with vegetable glycerin or apple cider vinegar). Consume 1/4 to 1 tsp three times daily. If using a commercial product, follow the instructions on the package. Black haw is a uterine relaxant and should be avoided while pregnant. It is also not recommended for those who suffer from kidney stones.

Black Walnut

Native to North America, this deciduous tree grows throughout the Central and Eastern regions of the United States. Known botanically as Juglans nigra, this tall tree with spicy-scented leaflets belongs to the Walnut family. The wood from the Black walnut tree and the large, hard nuts it produces are highly valued. The nuts are covered in thick husks that release a dark brown pigment, often used to make stains and dyes.

Historical/Traditional Uses: Black walnuts have long been used to treat hyperthyroidism, parasitic infections, headaches, toothaches, constipation, diarrhea, skin infections, and a host of other ailments[3][5][9][84]. The Cherokee relied on the inner bark to treat smallpox, while the Iroquois used it as an emetic and laxative[5].

Psychobotanical Uses: Rich in melatonin, polyphenols, folate, and vitamin E[25], research suggests that black walnuts contribute to improved brain health and overall cognitive functioning[34]. Animal studies show that it possesses sedating qualities comparable to diazepam[5]. Its chemical compounds help reduce irritability, manage over-excitability, and induce a sense of calm and relaxation. In addition, this plant is worth recommending for its neuroprotective properties[27].

Guidance: Black walnut hulls (outer coating of seed) and leaves are used medicinally for anxiety. For tea, add 1 tsp dried leaves to 1 cup boiling water. Steep for 10-20 minutes, strain, and drink up to one cup daily. For tincture, add 1 part dried hull to 5 parts 50% alcohol (may substitute with vegetable glycerin or apple cider vinegar). Consume 1 tsp three times daily. If using a commercial product, follow the instructions on the package.

Blessed Thistle

Also known as St. Benedict's Thistle, holy thistle, Centaurea benedicta, and spotted thistle, this hairy plant has been celebrated for its many uses. Known by the botanical name Cnicus benedictus, this annual plant is recognized by its yellow flowers, fibrous roots, and hairy/wooly leaves. Blessed Thistle belongs to the Asteraceae family and grows native to Europe and Asia. It thrives in open meadows and fields and has spread invasively worldwide.

Historical/Traditional Uses: Blessed Thistle has been used to treat a variety of ailments, including gastrointestinal pain, problems with appetite, digestion, breastmilk production, arthritis, respiration, and inflammation of the liver and gallbladder[5][9][44][84]. Other uses include its treatment for fevers, staunch bleeding, and memory problems. It is also recognized as the oldest known folk remedy for amenorrhea[96].

Psychobotanical Uses: A lesser-known utility of Blessed Thistle is its application in the treatment of anxiety-related symptoms. It can be used to manage irritability and improve mental clarity[6].

Guidance: Blessed Thistle flowers and leaves may be consumed medicinally. For tea, add 1 tsp of dried plant material to 1 cup of hot water for 10-15 minutes. Limit to one cup per day. For tincture, add 1 part dried leaves to 5 parts 45% alcohol (may substitute with vegetable glycerin or apple cider vinegar). Consume 1/2 to 1 tsp three times daily. Excessive use of this plant can lead to diarrhea, nausea, and vomiting. If using a commercial product, follow the instructions on the package. Must consult with a primary care doctor before use. This is especially necessary for pregnant women and people with inflammatory bowel diseases.

Blue Vervain/Common Vervain

F olk herbalists and healers have used this perennial flowering plant for thousands of years. Its two species, Verbena officinalis (European) and Verbena hastata (American), grow throughout North America, Africa, and Europe and thrive among prairies and meadows, stream banks, woodlands, and moist areas[18]. A member of the Verbenaceae family, this distinctive wildflower features oblong and lance-shaped leaves, erect stems, and vibrant violet blooms that attract a wide range of pollinators. Common names for this plant include Simpler's Joy, holy herb, Herb of the Cross, Herb of Grace, enchanter's herb, Indian hyssop, and Pigeon's Grass.

Historical/Traditional Uses: Both Vervain species are valued for their emetic, expectorant, anti-inflammatory, analgesic, antispasmodic, and diaphoretic properties. Haitian folk herbalists have long used Verbena officinalis to treat infections and rheumatism and as a blood tonic[95]. European herbalists applied it to treat fevers, acne, and kidney stones[15]. Nineteenth-century American physicians also administered it to treat fevers, intestinal parasites, and delayed menses[84].

Other uses included the treatment of inflammation, wounds, toothaches, headaches, asthma, and influenza. In France, Vervain is a popular after-dinner tisane (to stimulate digestion).

Psychobotanical Uses: When employed in treating anxiety, folk healers have utilized this plant to mitigate irritability, soothe anger, reduce muscle tension, and promote restful sleep[2][6]. It can "reign in the mind," "settle the body," uplift the mood, and promote optimism among sufferers of anxiety[12]. As a nervine and mild sedative, Vervain promotes relaxation[1][8], eases nervous tension[11], manages anger (mainly arising around the menstrual cycle)[8], and soothes restlessness[18]. It is also helpful in the management of panic symptoms[92], worrisome thoughts, and the nervous exhaustion that follows prolonged exposure to chronic stressors[8][11]. Haitian folk herbalists revere this plant as a calming tea for grief and managing intense emotional reactions[95].

Guidance: Vervain's aerial parts (flowers, stems, leaves) are used medicinally. Both fresh and dried plant material may be consumed in tea or tincture forms. For tea, add 1-3 tsp of plant material per cup of hot water. Steep for 20 minutes and drink 1-3 cups per day. For tincture, add 1 part fresh leaves and flower to 2 parts 60% alcohol (may substitute with vegetable glycerin or apple cider vinegar). If using dried leaves and flowers, add 1 part plant material to 5 parts 40% alcohol. Consume up to 1/2 tsp four times daily. If using a commercial product, follow the instructions on the package. Must consult a primary care doctor before use. Avoid while pregnant or nursing. Avoid use if diagnosed with chronic kidney disease or heart disease.

California Poppy

K nown by the botanical name Eschscholzia californica, this flowering plant is commonly referred to as Cup of Gold or Golden poppy. It is native to western North America and is widely cultivated in many parts of the world. California poppy is a member of the Papaveraceae (Poppy) family and is distinguished by its bright yellow, orange, and sometimes pinkish blooms.

Historical/Traditional Uses: California poppy has been historically used by Indigenous Americans for wound care, sleep problems[75], toothaches, and bedwetting in children[11]. In addition to its pain-relieving properties, this plant has been used to treat whooping cough and inflammation.

Psychobotanical Uses: When administered for mental health concerns, California poppy is extensively used as a mild anxiolytic, nervine, sedative, and sleep aid. Herbalists tout its ability to reduce irritability, agitation, muscle tension, restless legs, sleep disturbances, and psychological tension[2][9][11][92]. As a mild sedative, it helps calm the mind (without slowing down activity in the central nervous system) and promotes relaxation[3][8]. Unlike its close cousin opium, it is non-addictive. Nineteenth-century herbalists utilized this plant to promote calm sleep[84].

Guidance: The entire California poppy plant, or just the flowering tops and roots, may be used medicinally. Plant material is consumed in tea or tincture forms. For tea, add 1 tsp of California poppy to 1-2 cups of freshly boiling water. Steep for 10 minutes, strain, and drink. Tea may be consumed as needed. For tincture, add 1 part dried plant material to 5 parts 60% alcohol (may substitute with vegetable glycerin or apple cider vinegar). Consume 1/2 tsp daily as needed. Tinctures are far more effective than tea form. California poppy should be avoided during pregnancy or breastfeeding. Avoid driving or operating machinery after use. If using a commercial product, follow the instructions on the package. Consult with a primary care provider before use. This plant should not be combined with anti-anxiety or insomnia medications.

Canadian Wild Ginger

B otanically known as Asarum canadense, this perennial herb is recognizable by its waxy heart-shaped broad leaves, small reddish flowers, and creeping yellowish rhizomes. Part of the Birthwort family, it is low-growing and thrives as a floor cover in shaded forests, woodlands, and mountains.

Historical/Traditional Uses: Indigenous Americans have applied Canadian wild ginger to treat respiratory ailments, including asthma, pneumonia, and coughs. It was also administered for menstruation difficulties, liver disease, arrhythmia, rheumatism, fevers, headaches, and gastrointestinal problems.

Psychobotanical Uses: Canadian wild ginger also has a history of utilization for nervous conditions, including panic attacks, excitability, and irritability[5].

Guidance: Canadian wild ginger's root/rhizomes are used in medicinal concoctions. For tea, add tbsp of plant material to two cups of boiling water. Simmer on low heat for 20 minutes. Strain and let sit for five minutes before consuming. Drink 1-2 cups daily. Consult with a primary care doctor before use. This highly toxic plant should not be confused with commercially available ginger (commonly sold in grocery stores). Handle with caution and use only the root parts of the plant.

Cannabis

Botanically named Cannabis sativa, this popular plant has a long-established reputation for its pain-relieving properties[5][11]. Commonly known as marijuana, it belongs to the Hemp family and has been successfully cultivated worldwide. It is easily recognizable by its upright stalks and uniquely serrated leaves.

Historical/Traditional Uses: Cannabis has been historically valued for its fibers and medicinal properties. It was used throughout history to treat a host of conditions, including digestive ailments, catarrh, malaria, chronic pain, glaucoma, nausea, and female reproductive problems[5][11][90]. Cannabis is a known relaxant, analgesic, sedative, anti-emetic, and anti-inflammatory agent[11]. Other uses include its treatment for high cholesterol, circulatory problems, fibromyalgia, gout, migraines, and arthritis[96].

Psychobotanical Uses: There is evidence that cannabis was utilized in ancient times for its psychoactive properties[11][90]. Cannabis's whole leaves and extracts are frequently touted for their effects on anxious mood, racing thoughts, chronic worry, muscle tension, insomnia, stress-induced headaches, and a host of other anxiety-related symptomatology[5][11][96]. It can help alleviate anxiety in some people while increasing anxiety levels in others.

Guidance: Cannabis may be consumed in many forms, including extracts from its seeds, leaves, and flowering tops. The leaves may be smoked or consumed in tea form. Cannabidiol (CBD) extracts are also commercially available. If using a commercial product, follow the instructions on the package. High doses of cannabis can elicit euphoria, hallucinations, and heightened perceptual sensitivity[90]. There is also evidence that daily use leads to problems with motivation and deficits in learning and memory[58]. The movement to decriminalize cannabis has long been underway, and as of 2024, it has been legalized in most US states (as well as many countries around the world) for either recreational or medicinal use among adults. However, cannabis remains illegal under federal law in the United States.

Catnip

atmint, catswort, cat nep, field balm, nep, and herb
catta are among the countless names used to describe
this mild aromatic, perennial herb. It is identified by its heart-
shaped leaves, square branching stems, and small white
flowers with purple spots. Scientifically named Nepeta
cataria, this plant belongs to the Lamiaceae (Mint) family and
is native to the Mediterranean and Europe. Catnip is cultivated globally and thrives along roadsides and pathways, in
dry or mountain regions, and at high altitudes.

Historical/Traditional Uses: Catnip has been
used for thousands of years as a carminative, sedative, expectorant, and tranquilizer. It is a gentle remedy for digestive
problems, colds, fevers, colic, and chicken pox, and serves as a
uterine tonic for women's reproductive concerns (i.e., painful,
delayed, or irregular menses, pregnancy issues)[2][3][5][9][11][27]
[84]. Other uses include its application as an insect repellant,
digestive tonic, and influenza remedy[96].

Psychobotanical Uses: This nervine and mild sedative has been conventionally used to aid in relaxation[1][8] and
nervous agitation, as well as to help manage chronic worry/ap-

prehensive expectation[6]. As a "potent sleep inducer," it relieves insomnia, relaxes tight muscles, and calms the body (all without the residual effects of grogginess the following day)[1][3][9][15]. Nineteenth-century shakers touted this herb for its ability to treat nervous conditions,[19] and eclectic physicians extolled its use for "nervous irritability," "nervous headaches," and restlessness[57][84]. Herbalists have also promoted its ability to ameliorate digestive problems stemming from anxiety[3]. Catnip may be recommended to elevate mood[20], alleviate restlessness, resolve nightmares[75], and "quiet the mind"[5][6][96].

Guidance: Catnip's dried leaves, seeds, and flowering tops are gathered for medicinal uses. It may be consumed in tea or tincture forms. For tea, add 2 tsp of plant material to 1 cup of hot water and let infuse for 15 minutes. Drink 1-3 cups per day. For tincture, add 1 part dried plant material to 5 parts 50% alcohol (may substitute with vegetable glycerin or apple cider vinegar). Consume 1 tsp up to three times daily. If using a commercial product, follow the instructions on the package.

Chamomile (German & Roman/English)

This widely popular and celebrated flowering plant grows abundantly in many parts of the world. More than 4,000 tons are grown worldwide each year. The two species commonly used in herbalism (German and Roman/English) are scientifically known as Matricaria recutita and Chamaemelum nobile and native to Asia and Europe. Common names for this plant include wild chamomile, mayweed, earth apple, mantazilla, and "physical plant" (due to its ability to improve the health of plants around it). Both species are distinguished by their white daisy-like flowers with yellow centers, and the Roman species produces the scent of fresh green apples. They belong to the Asteraceae family.

Historical/Traditional Uses: Chamomile has long been used as a gentle calmative[6], sedative, digestive tonic[5][8] [10], carminative[6][9], muscle relaxant[10][14], anti-inflammatory agent, and sleep aid[9]. It has been administered to treat everything from gout, diarrhea, and colic to sciatica, headaches, and colds/flu[5][8][75]. It was also utilized as a "strewing herb" (an herb used to mask foul odors) due to the pleasantness of its natural aroma[1].

Psychobotanical Uses: This relatively small and fragrant nervine is often recommended for people experiencing insomnia[1][6][10][92], irritability[9][11], hyperactivity[9], muscle tension[10][11][92], restlessness[2], anxious mood[1][15][27], and anxiety-induced gastrointestinal issues[3][11][13][15][75]. It can help ease stress and agitation[92], settle the mind, and improve levels of distress tolerance[12]. It has also been promoted for its ability to alleviate gastrointestinal symptoms associated with anxiety. Chamomile serves as a nervine, hypnotic, tranquilizing, and calming herb[1] that is especially helpful in the case of mild anxiety and nervousness[10][14][15][65]. Shaker healers from the 19th century celebrated this herb for its ability to treat "hysteria and nervousness"[19]. African American folk healers utilized this herb as a general calming tonic[27]. Clinical studies have shown significant reductions in anxiety symptoms among adults who took 1,100 mg of chamomile extract daily for eight weeks[15]. Laboratory studies have also demonstrated that inhaling essential oils can reduce the production of stress hormones and even improve the effectiveness of anti-anxiety medication[3].

Guidance: Chamomile's dried or fresh flower heads are used in medicinal teas and tinctures. To maximize the plant's medicinal effects, pick flowers during the summer months while in full bloom. For tea, add 1 tbsp of dried flowerheads and leaves to 150 mL of hot water, cover, and steep for 10-15 minutes. Strain and drink up to 2-3 cups per day. For tincture, add 1 part plant material to 5 parts 45% alcohol (may substitute with vegetable glycerin or apple cider vinegar). Consume 2 tsp up to 3 times daily. Chamomile contains natural blood thinners, so avoid it while taking prescription blood thinners. Those who suffer from known ragweed allergies should avoid use. If using a commercial product, follow the instructions on the package.

. . .

Chinese Polygala

This perennial herb is known botanically as Polygala tenuifolia, grows native to Asia, and belongs to the Milkwort family (i.e., relatives of legumes, peas, and beans). Commonly called "Yuan zhi," it can be recognized by its thin stems, slender roots, and small, three-petaled flowers.

Historical/Traditional Uses: Chinese herbalists traditionally revered this pungent and bitter herb as a general tonic, expectorant, and tranquilizer. It is used in traditional Chinese medicine to combat Alzheimer's disease, age-related cognitive decline, neurasthenia, and disorientation [9][94]. It is also used as a kidney tonic.

Psychobotanical Uses: Herbalists have relied on Chinese polygala for the treatment of anxiety, depression, and fear-related symptoms[8][11]. Research supports its ability to reduce anxious and depressed mood, manage intense fearfulness, reduce anxiety-induced heart palpitations, limit stress-induced memory loss, minimize sleep disturbances, alleviate restlessness, and inhibit the body's release of cortisol[8][94]. Chinese polygala is reputedly stronger than many anxiolytics on the market[8].

59

Guidance: Chinese polygala's dried root is consumed medicinally. For tea, add 3/4 tsp to one cup of boiling water. Simmer for 20-30 minutes, strain, and drink one cup twice daily. For tincture, add 1 part root to 5 parts 50% alcohol (may substitute with vegetable glycerin or apple cider vinegar). Consume 1/2 tsp up to 3 times daily. Consult with a primary care doctor before use. Large doses may lead to nausea and vomiting. If using a commercial product, follow the instructions on the package.

Codonopsis

This adaptogenic herb is native to northeastern China and extensively cultivated worldwide[3][11]. Known scientifically as Codonopsis pilosula, this shade-loving plant can be recognized by its lovely bell-shaped flowers with purple veins and trailing vines. Codonopsis belongs to the Campanulaceae family of plants.

Historical/Traditional Uses: Codonopsis was utilized as a general tonic that improves well-being, boosts stamina, and increases energy levels[11]. It is also said to improve appetite, relieve digestive problems, increase breast-milk production, strengthen immune functioning, and aid with respiratory issues. Codonopsis helps increase red blood cells and is even helpful in reducing some of the side effects of chemotherapy and radiation[9].

Psychobotanical Uses: When applied to the management of anxiety, Codonopsis aids in mitigating nervous exhaustion, chronic stress, tension headaches, irritability, and muscle tension[3][11].

Guidance: Codonopis root is used in herbal remedies. For tea, add 2 tsp of root to 1 cup of boiling water. Simmer for 20-30 minutes and allow to cool for 10 minutes. Consume up to three cups daily. For tincture, add 1 part root to 3 parts 50% alcohol (may substitute with vegetable glycerin or apple cider vinegar). Consume 1/2 tsp up to 4 times daily.

Corydalis

Scientifically named Corydalis yanhusuo, this perennial flowering plant has long been used for its pain-relieving/analgesic properties[9][11]. Native to China, Japan, and the Siberian region, it thrives in shaded woodlands and forest areas. Due to its lovely clusters of pink flowers and narrow fern-like leaves, Corydalis is also cultivated for ornamental gardens. It belongs to the Papaveraceae (Poppy) family.

Historical/Traditional Uses: Herbalists have valued Corydalis for its ability to treat abdominal and chest pain, reduce menstrual cramps, and slow the formation of cataracts[3][11]. It is generally helpful for pain associated with arthritis, rheumatism, and menstruation[9].

Psychobotanical Uses: Applied to anxiety, Corydalis is administered for its hypnotic, sedating, and tranquilizing properties[3]. It helps treat anxious mood, insomnia, restlessness, nervousness, and psychomotor agitation [3][9][11]. A laboratory study on tetrahydroprotoberberines (an isolated alkaloid found in Corydalis), demonstrated this herb's anxiolytic effects[49][75].

Guidance: Corydalys's root and dried rhizomes are

63

used in medicinal remedies (in powder form). This plant is typically combined with other herbs to maximize benefits. Consume dried rhizomes in tincture fork (tea is not advised due to its unpleasant taste). For tincture, add 1 part dried plant material to 3 parts 50% alcohol (may substitute with vegetable glycerin or apple cider vinegar). Consume 1 tsp daily as needed. If using a commercial product, follow the instructions on the package.

Cramp Bark

This deciduous flowering shrub is native to North Africa, North Asia, and Europe. Botanically named Viburnum opulus, it thrives in the woodlands and thickets of these regions and flowers during the summer months. Cramb bark is characterized by its cranberry-like fruit, 3-lobed leaves, and white flowers. It is a close relative of Blackhaw, and sometimes, it is used interchangeably. It belongs to the Adoxaceae family.

Historical/Traditional Uses: Cramp bark was historically utilized by the indigenous people of North America to treat eye ailments, fever, and gastrointestinal issues. As a strong antispasmodic, it was relied upon to treat cramps and spasms of all kinds, including menstrual cramps and "spasmodic contractions of the bladder"[9][84]. Other uses include the treatment of gynecological problems, pregnancy-induced epilepsy, and miscarriage[84].

Psychobotanical Uses: As a mild sedative and relaxant, cramp bark helps manage some of the physical manifestations of anxiety, including symptoms of muscle tension, spasms, and breathing difficulties[9][11][96]. It is also useful in treating insomnia[96].

Guidance: Cramp bark's fresh and dried bark, as well as the berries, are used medicinally. For tea, add 2 tsp of plant material to 1 cup of boiling water. Gently simmer for 20 minutes. Consume 1 cup three times daily. For tincture, add 1 part dried bark to 5 parts 50% alcohol (may substitute with vegetable glycerin or apple cider vinegar). Consume 1 tsp up to four times daily.

Cucumber Magnolia

Scientifically named Magnolia acuminata, this deciduous tree grows throughout eastern North America, from New York to Georgia. A member of the Magnolia family, it is commonly referred to as cucumber tree, blue magnolia, or mountain magnolia. Cucumber magnolia is distinguished by its bluish and yellowish flowers, cucumber-like cones, and oval, acuminate leaves.

Historical/Traditional Uses: Unlike its southern magnolia cousin, Cucumber magnolia's medicinal bark was extensively used by Indigenous people and eclectic physicians of North America. The Iroquois and Cherokee used this plant to treat malaria, typhoid fever, rheumatism, digestive problems, parasitic infections, and toothaches[5][84].

Psychobotanical Uses: Herbalists have touted magnolia bark for its sedating effects, including its ability to reduce sleep disturbances, lower stress hormones (i.e., cortisol), and minimize transitory anxiety.

Guidance: The bark of Cucumber magnolia is used in medicinal remedies, especially tea. For tea, add 2 tsp of dried bark per 1 cup of boiling water. Gently simmer for 25-35 minutes. Consume 1 cup twice daily. If using a commercial product, follow the instructions on the package.

Damiana

This perennial shrub, with its small yellow flowers, grows in dry sandy or rocky regions of the United States, Mexico, Namibia, Central and South Americas, and northern parts of the Caribbean. It is botanically known as Turnera diffusa (Turneraceae family) and commonly known as Mexican holly and 'old woman's broom.' It can be identified by its small, single yellow flowers, smooth leaves with serrated edges, and spicy aroma.

Historical/Traditional Uses: The Mayans have used Damiana as an aphrodisiac for thousands of years. It was also conventionally used as a diuretic, laxative, flavoring agent, and to manage painful or delayed menses[6][11][16][84]. Early herbalists also promoted its use as a digestive tonic and emetic[84].

Psychobotanical Uses: Damiana also boasts many mental health benefits. It is a celebrated nerve tonic that aids with anxiety symptoms, including irritability, tension, stress, and nervous exhaustion[9][11][16][92]. Damiana also helps improve sleep and induce a calming and euphoric emotional state[35]. It is ideal for people who may be experiencing depression and anxiety simultaneously[11][92].

Guidance: Damiana's fresh and dried leaves are the parts used medicinally. For tea, brew 1-2 tsp of dried leaves in 1 cup of water. Limit to 4 cups per day. For tincture, add 1 part dried leaves to 5 parts 60% alcohol (may substitute with vegetable glycerin or apple cider vinegar). Consume 1 tsp up to four times daily. Note: Damiana may decrease fertility during use. If using a commercial product, follow the instructions on the package. Consult with a primary care doctor before use.

Dropwort

Also known as fern-leaf dropwort and meadowsweet, this perennial herb is native to Eurasia, parts of Northern Africa, and the Middle East. It thrives in marshlands and meadows, along streams banks, and in forests. Botanically known as Filipendula vulgaris, it is now cultivated worldwide for its medicinal purposes, ecological value, and aesthetic value (i.e., for ornamental gardens). A member of the Rose family, it is recognizable by its eye-catching clusters of white flowers that emit a sweet and delicate almond-like fragrance.

Historical/Traditional Uses: Dropwort was prized as an effective diuretic, astringent, analgesic, anti-inflammatory agent, and remedy for gastrointestinal problems (e.g., indigestion, diarrhea, nausea)[14][15]. Folk healers also relied upon this herb as a remedy for fevers, colds, coughs, and headaches[5][15], as well as gynecological problems (e.g., vaginal discharge, cramps)[15]. It was also utilized as a "strewing herb" (an herb used to mask foul odors) due to the pleasantness of its natural aroma[1].

Psychobotanical Uses: While there is limited information and research on the psychotherapeutic benefits of Dropwort, herbalists have found it helpful in the treatment of anxiety. Its calming effect on the central nervous system induces relaxation and relieves tension in the body.

Guidance: Dropwort's aerial parts (flowering tops and leaves) are used medicinally. It may be consumed as leaf tea or extract. The leaf extract is said to be stronger than valerian root[5]. For tea, add 1 tbsp of dried flowering tops and leaves to one cup of hot water, cover, and steep for 15-20 minutes. Strain and drink up to 2-3 cups per day. Consult with a primary care doctor before use. Avoid while taking blood thinners. If using a commercial product, follow the instructions on the package.

Echinacea

This perennial herb is native to North America and grows abundantly in wooded regions and open prairies. Nine species of Echinacea have been identified, but only three are used medicinally[14][17]. They include Echinacea angustifolia, Echinacea purpurea, and Echinacea pallida, known commonly as Eastern purple coneflower, Indian snakeroot, black Sampson, red sunflower, and Indian head. The name 'echinacea' comes from the Greek word "echinos", which describes the herb's spiny seed head (resembling a hedgehog or sea urchin).

Echinacea is easy to spot, with its daisy-like flowerhead with cone-shaped centers, purple rays, hairy leaves, and single upright stems. A member of the Sunflower family, it attracts a wide range of pollinators (i.e., butterflies, bees, and birds) and makes a wonderful addition to ornamental gardens.

Historical/Traditional Uses: Indigenous American healers used Echinacea to treat various conditions. It was revered as a painkiller (especially for toothaches), eyewash, cough suppressant, wound cleanser, acne treatment, cold/flu remedy, and to treat highly contagious infectious diseases (i.e., smallpox and measles)[1][2][5][16][17][18]. African Americens enslaved on plantations in Georgia, Texas, and North Carolina utilized Echinaceae to treat cramps, stomach pain, and joint pain[103]. Other uses include its treatment for snake and insect bites[3][5][11][84], septicemia, malaria, tonsillitis, impotence[84], skin abrasions, and ulcerations[14][59], to boost the body's natural immunity[3][10][16], and prevent infections of the urinary, gynecologic, respiratory, and digestive systems[1][11][15]. Nineteenth-century eclectic physicians also utilized it for pain management among patients with cancer[84]. Modern day herbalists in Nigeria utilize Echinacea as a remedy for influenza[59].

Psychobotanical Uses: Modern herbalists administer Echinacea purpurea and Echinacea angustifolia to treat anxiety and anxiety-related symptoms[2][17]. A double-blind clinical study on Echinacea angustifolia root extract found that adults who took 80 mg a day for seven weeks experienced significant reductions in "state anxiety" (anxiety in response to specific situations or moments)[50]. Echinacea helps manage tension headaches, chronic fear, nervousness, and hyper-aroused states.

Guidance: Echinacea root is traditionally used for medicinal purposes, but many argue that the aerial (above ground) parts are also beneficial[14]. It may be consumed in tea or tincture forms. For tea, add 2 tsp plant material per cup of boiling water. Drink one cup three times daily. For tincture, add 1 part dried plant material to 5 parts 60% alcohol (may substitute with vegetable glycerin or apple cider vinegar). Consume 1 tsp four times per day. If using a commercial product, follow the instructions on the package.

Egyptian/Blue Lotus

T he early Egyptians venerated this aquatic perennial as a symbol of creation, rebirth, and continual renewal. Early depictions of this plant can be found on ancient Egyptian papyri and along tombs dating back to the 14[th]century B.C. Known as the blue lotus flower, blue water lily, and sacred blue lily, it features a sizeable star-shaped flower with golden stamens surrounded by light blue petals. Egyptian blue lotus is native to the Northern and Central African regions and can be found floating along ponds, riverbanks, muddy shallow waters, and slow-moving streams. Botanically, it is known as Nymphaea caerulea and belongs to the Nymphaeaceae family of water lilies.

Historical/Traditional Uses: Egyptian blue lotus is a versatile herb that offers a wide range of traditional uses. Ancient Egyptians revered this plant as a potent natural hypnotic, stimulant, sedative, and aphrodisiac. It was also heavily utilized in magical/spiritual ceremonies, including burial rites.

Psychobotanical Uses: Egyptian blue lotus is an adaptogen and nervine that can relieve stress, elicit relaxation, ease anxiety, and promote sleep among anxiety sufferers. In traditional Chinese medicine, it has been used to treat restlessness and insomnia and to "quiet the spirits"[75]. It also contains chemical compounds that have been used to treat erectile dysfunction, depression, schizophrenia, and motor deficits. Previous laboratory studies have demonstrated the significant anxiolytic effect of its leaf extract[98].

Guidance: The entire plant can be used in medicinal remedies (i.e., flowers, fruit, tubers, leaves, rhizomes, roots, and seeds). It may be consumed in tea and tincture forms. For tea, add 1-2 tsp plant material per cup of boiling water. Drink one cup daily. Consult with a primary care doctor before use.

Eleuthero

K nown commonly as Siberian ginseng, this hardy deciduous shrub can be found in the mountain forests of Asia and Russia. Scientifically named Eleutherococcus senticosus, it is a member of the Araliaceae family (and commonly confused with American and Chinese Ginseng (though it has many ginseng-like qualities).

Historical/Traditional Uses: Eleuthero has been used in China as a memory aid, appetite stimulant, and general tonic for thousands of years[14]. In more recent history, it was popularized as a physical and cognitive performance enhancer[11]. Russian scientists administered Eleuthero as a "training aid" for the 1972 through 1994 Olympic athletes[3] [13][14]. At the time, it was thought to help increase physical functioning by improving stamina and endurance, reducing fatigue, and increasing stress tolerance after workouts[11]. News of its benefits spread, and everyone quickly adopted it, from soldiers and astronauts[11] to musicians and chess players seeking an edge against their competitors[3]. Other uses include it treatment of bronchitis, hypertension, and hyper-lipidemia[96].

Psychobotanical Uses: Eleuthero continues to be promoted as an adaptogen that helps with anxiety, concentration, insomnia, and recovery from exposure to chronic stress[2] [11][92]. Several herbalists promote it as an ideal herb for driven, Type A personalities who find it difficult to slow down[8][92]. Studies suggest that Eleuthero increases one's resistance to stress and decreases activation of the adrenal cortex (which controls vital organ functions)[3][14]. Among Chinese healers, it is valued as an effective remedy for insomnia[96].

Guidance: Eleuthero's dried root is most commonly used for remedies. It may be consumed in tea, tincture, capsules, or powder forms. For tea, add 2-4 grams to 1 cup of freshly boiling water. Steep for 1 hour, strain, and drink up to 3 cups daily. For tincture, add 1 part dried root to 5 parts 60% alcohol (may substitute with vegetable glycerin or apple cider vinegar). Consume 1 to 2 tsp daily. If using a commercial product, follow the instructions on the package. Consult with a primary care doctor before use. It is not recommended for people who struggle with insomnia.

European Bugleweed

Also known as Gypsywort and waterhorehound, this perennial herb thrives best in moist/wet environments (especially around lakes, rivers, streams, ditches, and marshes). Native to Europe and Asia, it can now be found spreading along the Eastern regions of North America. Botanically named Lycopus europaeus (Mint family), it can be recognized by its slender and elongated leaves, serrated edges, and small clusters of white flowers that attract pollinators.

Historical/Traditional Uses: European bugleweed has long been used to treat hyperthyroidism, anxiety, and heart palpitations[5]. It was also administered to treat pulmonary complaints and gastrointestinal conditions[84].

Psychobotanical Uses: Eclectic physicians of the late 19th century touted European bugleweed's ability to manage anxiety, irritability, insomnia, and "morbid vigilance"[84]. There is a possibility that this herb only treats anxiety that is secondary to an overactive thyroid. The King's American Dispensatory described this herb as a quick remedy for "the suffering and anxiety nearly always experienced in heart disease"[84].

Guidance: European bugleweed's aerial parts are used medicinally. For tea, add 1 tsp of fresh plant material to one cup of boiling water. Steep for 15-25 minutes, then drink 1-3 times daily. Consult with a primary care doctor before use. It may increase thyroid size and is contraindicated in moderate to severe coronary artery disease. Avoid use while pregnant or nursing. If using a commercial product, follow the instructions on the package.

Figwort

Commonly referred to as Carpenter's square or Maryland figwort, this herb grows abundantly throughout eastern and central North America. Known botanically as Scrophularia marilandica, Figwort thrives in rich woodlands and thickets. It is characterized by small tubular flowers and hairy stems, with either toothy or serrated leaves. Its heavy nectar attracts pollinators, including bees, butterflies, and birds. Figwort belongs to the Scrophulariaceae family.

Historical/Traditional Uses: Figwort has been utilized as a diuretic, tonic, fever-reducer, emmenagogue, and to treat ringworms and hemorrhoids. It was reputedly beneficial in treating liver and kidney problems in the early twentieth century[84].

Psychobotanical Uses: Applied to mental health, this herb has been lauded for its ability to treat anxiety-related symptoms, including anxious mood, insomnia, and restlessness[5].

Guidance: Figwort's leaves and root are used medicinally. For tea, add 1 tbsp of plant material per cup of water. Boil for 20-30 minutes and drink up to three times daily. If using a commercial product, follow the instructions on the package.

Gardenia

This fragrant shrub has long been celebrated for its beautiful double flowers and pleasant scent. Known scientifically as Gardenia jasminoides, it belongs to the Rubiaceae family (the same as coffee). Native to the Southeastern regions of China, gardenia has been used in Chinese medicine for over 2,000 years[11].

Historical/Traditional Uses: Gardenia is widely used in herbal formulas that treat everything from fevers and constipation, to bacterial infections and hypertension[3]. In traditional Chinese medicine, it has been used to treat cystitis, painful urination, jaundice, and to staunch excessive bleeding of the nose, rectum, and urinary tract[11].

Psychobotanical Uses: Gardenia fruit can help anxiety sufferers manage restlessness, irritability, and insomnia[11]. Animal studies also showed that inhaling Gardenia essential oil had a significant anxiolytic effect[52].

Guidance: The Gardenia fruit is used medicinally. It may be eaten directly or brewed in tea. For tea, add 1-2 tsp of plant material to one cup of boiled water. Steep and cover for

15-20 minutes. Drink up to three cups daily. Avoid while taking hypertension medication.

Ginkgo

Known commonly as the Maidenhair tree and 'Autumn gold,' this ornamental perennial has long been regarded as the world's oldest known tree on the earth (existing more than 200 million years)[5][11][14][17]. A single ginkgo tree can live up to a thousand years[3]. Known scientifically as Ginkgo biloba (Ginkgo family), it is native to China and has been extensively cultivated throughout many parts of the world. Ginkgo can be recognized by its tall and upright stature, broad spread, unique fan-shaped leaves, and almond-like seeds. The foliage takes on a distinct and stunning golden hue during autumn.

Historical/Traditional Uses: Ginkgo is the most widely used treatment for memory loss, to improve blood flow to the brain, and to manage other neurodegenerative conditions[3]. Herbalists have applied leaf extract to treat dementia, circulatory problems[16], traumatic brain injury[14], lung ailments[5], vertigo[9], tinnitus[17], and erectile dysfunction[15].

Psychobotanical Uses: Ginkgo leaves contain medicinal compounds that help manage anxiety-related symptoms. Among anxiety sufferers, it can improve cognitive functioning and reduce distress, irritability, apathy, indifference, insomnia, and lability[3][13]. A study conducted among older adults found that those who took a daily dose of of 480 mg of Ginkgo showed significant reductions in anxiety after four weeks[15].

Guidance: Ginkgo leaves and seeds are used in medicinal preparations. For tea, add 2 tsp plant material (or 3-4 seeds) to 1 pint of hot water. Drink one cup three times daily. For tincture, consume 25-50 drops 1-3 times/day. If using a commercial extract, follow the instructions on the package. Consult with a primary care doctor before use. Avoid while taking blood thinners or medication for diabetes and hypertension.

Gotu Kola

This creeping perennial is commonly referred to as Indian pennywort or Asiatic pennywort. Gotu Kola is native to India and the southern region of the United States and has been used by Ayurvedic healers for thousands of years[3]. It is currently cultivated throughout the world, from Southern Africa to Australia. Gotu Kola is characterized by its smooth and kidney-shaped leaves, small bunches of pink or flowers, and tendency to grow low to the ground. Its rhizomes grow aggressively in moist, shaded areas. It is scientifically referred to as Centella asiatica and is a member of the Apiaceae family.

Historical/Traditional Uses: Gotu Kola was widely used by Ayurvedic doctors for thousands of years[3]. It was employed in the treatment of leprosy, skin abrasions, ulcerations[84], fevers, upper respiratory infections, circulatory problems, memory loss, and age-related cognitive decline[15] [96]. It is lauded as an adaptogen and general tonic that can improve longevity and vitality.

Psychobotanical Uses: Several studies indicate that Gotu Kola may help relieve a host of mental health symptoms, including problems with anxiety, memory, and attention[11]. Other researchers found this herb helpful in significantly improving mood and reducing reactivity to stress (i.e., decreased startle responses[15]). Gotu Kola promotes relaxation,

Guidance: Gotu Kola's dried and fresh leaves are used medicinally. It may be consumed in tea or tincture form. For tea, add 1/2 tsp dried leaves per cup of boiling water. Drink one cup daily. For tincture, add 1 part dried root to 5 parts 60% alcohol (may substitute with vegetable glycerin or apple cider vinegar). Consume 1/2 tsp 2-4 times daily. If using a commercial product, follow the instructions on the package. Pregnant women and people with hyperthyroidism should avoid use.

Hawthorn

This polyonymous shrub goes by many names, including English hawthorn, midland hawthorn, maybush, may tree, haw, quickset, thornapple, whitethorn, cockspur, red haw, summer haw, cockspur thorn, and Washington thorn. The species most commonly utilized in herbal medicine are Crataegus oxyacantha and Crataegus laveigata (Rose family). They may be identified by their beautiful clusters of large flowers, edible red berries, and protective woody thorns. Hawthorn can be found along roadsides, thickets, and fields throughout the northern hemisphere and the British Isles[11].

Historical/Traditional Uses: Hawthorn is primarily known for its ability to treat cardiac and circulatory problems[3][9][84]. It was commonly administered to treat arrhythmia, congestive heart failure, angina, and a host of other heart conditions[96]. Herbalists have included Hawthorn in herbal remedies for asthma, diabetes, and kidney stones[14].

Psychobotanical Uses: A lesser-known benefit is Hawthorn's effect on mood. A small double-blind study found that adults who consumed an herbal supplement with Hawthorn experienced significant reductions in anxiety ratings[55]. As a nervine, this herb soothes chronic stress, mental agitation, restlessness, and somatic complaints related to anxiety[2][5][15].

Guidance: Hawthorn's flowering tops, leaves, berries, and bark have been celebrated for their healing properties[14]. It may be consumed in tea or tincture forms. For tea, add 2 tsp plant material per cup of boiling water. Drink 1 cup three times daily. For tincture, add 1 part plant material to 5 parts 45% alcohol (may substitute with vegetable glycerin or apple cider vinegar). Consume 1 tsp three times daily. If using a commercial extract, follow the instructions on the package. Consult with a primary care doctor before use.

Holy Basil

This highly-revered and sacred herb belongs to the Lamiaceae (Mint) family and is said to have over 3,000 years of recorded medicinal use[10]. Holy Basil has many names, including Tulsi, Tulasi, Ocimum sanctum, Indian basil, "queen of herbs," sacred basil, hot basil, and "the incomparable one." Botanically named Ocimum tenuiflorum, it is native to India and extensively cultivated throughout Central and South America, as well as the Northeastern regions of Africa. It can be recognized by its small purple and white flowers, fuzzy leaves with serrated edges,

Historical/Traditional Uses: In India, Holy basil is traditionally used for spiritual/religious rites and is commonly planted around sacred temples and courtyards[2] [11]. Spiritual yogis who wanted to "embrace enlightenment" also utilized this herb[43]. Like its close relative, sweet basil, it is a popular culinary herb. Medicinally, Holy basil has a long-standing history of use as a general tonic that restores and rejuvenates the body. Herbalists relied on it to treat hypertension, hypercholesterolemia, high blood sugar, bronchitis, asthma, and fevers[9][11].

Psychobotanical Uses: As an adaptogen, Holy basil helps people achieve relaxation, manage anxious mood, control "mental fog," reduce stress, and minimize cognitive deficits due to anxiety[92]. It restores the body by improving adaptation to stressors and new demands[11][43]. Promising results have come out of preliminary investigations into its use for stress-related memory, sexual, and sleep problems[43]. It is also helpful to those experiencing anticipatory or performance anxiety while facing new challenges[2]. A clinical trial on 35 adult patients who received 1,000 mg of Holy basil leaf extract showed significant improvements in generalized anxiety symptoms[99].

Guidance: Holy basil's dried and fresh aerial parts are used medicinally (and picked before the flowers open). For tea, add 1 tsp dried leaves to 8 ounces of hot water and steep for 5-10 minutes. Consume up to 4 cups daily. For tincture, add 1 part plant material to 5 parts 60% alcohol (may substitute with vegetable glycerin or apple cider vinegar). Consume 1 tsp three times daily. Consult with a primary care doctor before use. This herb may reduce fertility during use. If using a commercial product, follow the instructions on the package.

Hops

This hairy, climbing perennial vine has been widely used to brew beer throughout the ages. The name is derived from the Anglo-Saxon word "hoppan," which means "to climb". Known scientifically as Humulus lupulus, hops are found in the marshy regions of the United States and along roadsides, hedges, and open areas in Europe and Asia. It belongs to the Hemp/Cannabaceae family and can be identified by its layered, cone-like strobiles.

Historical/Traditional Uses: Hops have been traditionally used as a mild sedative, diuretic, digestive stimulant, and antispasmodic[5][11][14][15]. Folk herbalists employed this plant to treat many conditions, ranging from insomnia, digestive problems, and asthma to fevers, tuberculosis, and rheumatism[5][15][16]. Hops is also a known pain reliever and digestive aid[96].

Psychobotanical Uses: A lesser-known benefit of hops is its use as a mild sedative, calmative, and hypnotic that aids in the treatment of anxiety and insomnia[3][8][14]. Among anxiety sufferers, hops may help manage irritability[9][14], excitability[11], agitation[14], tension[16], restlessness[11][84], stress-induced insomnia[9][75], heart palpitations[14], nervousness[5][6] and digestive problems[75]. Herbalists rely on hops to calm the mind and body by quieting racing thoughts and relaxing the muscles[6]. The German Commission E, a scientific advisory board formed in 1978, approved Hops for treating anxiety and sleep disorders[65]. Nineteenth-century herbalists also touted its ability to manage chronic restlessness, "morbid excitement," and vigilance[84].

Guidance: Hops strobiles (i.e., the scaly catkins from female flowers) are the parts most often used for medicine. As the herb dries and ages, concentrations of its active ingredients increase. When allowed to age for two years, it creates a chemical compound similar to chlordiazepoxide and diazepam (widely used anxiety medications)[3]. Hops may be consumed in tea or tincture forms. For tea, add 2 tsp plant material per cup of boiling water. Drink one cup three times daily. For tincture, add 1 part plant material to 5 parts 60% alcohol (may substitute with vegetable glycerin or apple cider vinegar). Consume 1/2 tsp three times daily, with the final dose before bedtime. If using a commercial product, follow the instructions on the package. It is not recommended for those with a history of depression.

Indian Pipe

Also known as ghost plant or ghost pipe, this perennial herb grows in dark, shaded forests throughout North America. As the name implies, Indian-pipe is recognized by its uniquely pale, white, and translucent petals and stalk (resembling a "ghost" in the dark). Scientifically named Monotropa uniflora (Heath family), it is native to North America and increasingly rare in the wild.

Historical/Traditional Uses: Indigenous peoples of North America traditionally used Indian-pipe to treat a host of conditions. The Mohegans relied on it for its analgesic properties, while the Cherokee used it to treat epileptic seizures, eye inflammation, and various skin conditions[5]. Eclectic physicians of the early 20th century regarded it as a tonic, diaphoretic, and antispasmodic[84]. It was employed to treat pain, fevers, ulcers, and gonorrhea.

Psychobotanical Uses: Recognized as a nervine and mild sedative, early herbalists used Indian-pipe to manage nervous irritability and restlessness[84]. Reputedly, it can also help treat panic-like symptoms[9].

Guidance: Indian-pipe's aerial parts are used for medicinal purposes. For tincture, add 1 part plant material to 2 parts 95% alcohol (may substitute with vegetable glycerin or apple cider vinegar). Consume 1/2 tsp as needed. If using a commercial product, follow the instructions on the package.

Indian Tobacco

This herbaceous plant can be found throughout the Eastern and Central regions of the United States and Canada. Known botanically as Lobelia inflata, Indian tobacco may be identified by its inflated seed pods, pale blue flowers, and ovate leaves. It belongs to the Bellflower family and grows in open fields, woods, and waste places.

Historical/Traditional Uses: Commonly referred to as Puke weed and gagroot, the plant was widely used by Indigenous Americans to induce vomiting (notably because it causes significant nausea when ingested in large amounts)[14]. It was also utilized as an expectorant in the treatment of respiratory conditions (i.e., asthma, bronchitis, coughs), and as a remedy for skin diseases, sore throat, and fever[5][84]. African American folk healers relied on this plant in the treatment of fevers[82]. Indian tobacco was once considered the 'herb of choice' for cardiac and thoracic pain[84].

Psychobotanical Uses: In the treatment of anxiety, early 20th-century folk healers utilized Indian tobacco as a relaxant, antispasmodic, nervine, and sedative. It was used to relax nerves, reduce muscle spasms and tension[14], and treat insomnia[82][91]. It has also been promoted for its euphoric effects, treatment of nervousness, and anxiety-induced heart palpitations[75]. More research is needed to support its safety and efficacy in the treatment of anxiety.

Guidance: Dried Indian tobacco leaves are smoked or consumed as liquid extract or tincture for medicinal purposes. For tincture, add 1 part dried plant material to 5 parts 65% alcohol (may substitute with vegetable glycerin or apple cider vinegar). Consume 1/4 tsp as needed. This plant contains poisonous, toxic alkaloids and is potentially fatal (i.e., fatal overdoses have been reported throughout history[9][14][18]). If using a commercial product, follow the instructions on the package. Consult with a primary care doctor before use. Avoid if diagnosed with cardiovascular or respiratory diseases.

Jamaican Dogwood

This flowering deciduous tree is commonly known as Jamaican dogwood and botanically known as Piscidia erythrina (a member of the Legume family). It is native to Jamaica, Haiti, southern Florida, and Central and South America. Fishermen traditionally used Jamaican dogwood to stun/stupefy fish before catching them. It can be identified by its light pink flowers, smooth gray bark, and distinctive leaf color (leaf topside dark green, underside grayish green).

Historical/Traditional Uses: Jamaican dogwood is highly recognized for its strong sedating and analgesic effects[8][84]. Historically, it has been used to treat rheumatism, whooping cough, delayed or irregular menses, and bronchitis[60]. Herbalists also tout its ability to manage nerve pain[8] and hypertension[75].

Psychobotanical Uses: When applied to anxiety, it has long been utilized in the management of nervous tension, irritability, chronic stress, and stress-induced insomnia[9]. It treats over-excitability[84], muscle spasms[75], and mental hyperactivity[11]. Early 20th-century eclectic physicians extolled its ability to help patients relieve distress, slow the pulse, and achieve restful sleep, especially "when the insomnia is due to nervous excitement, mental worry or anxiety"[60][75]. Jamaican dogwood is also helpful in treating anxiety-induced hypertension[75].

Guidance: Jamaican dogwood's tree bark is used in medicinal preparations. For tincture, add 1 part dried bark to 5 parts 80% alcohol (may substitute with vegetable glycerin or apple cider vinegar). Consume 1/2 tsp three times daily. If using a commercial product, follow the instructions on the package.

Kava

This perennial shrub has been traditionally used by the Indigenous people of Polynesia and the Pacific Islands for over 3,000 years. With heart-shaped leaves, it has a long-standing history of cultural, spiritual, economic, and ecological significance to the people of this region. From deaths to marriages, or just as a means to bond over conversation, Kava is utilized in various community events and daily rituals. It is known botanically as Macropiper methysticum and falls under the Piperaceae family (a relative of black pepper).

Kava ceremony in Fiji

Historical/Traditional Uses: Herbalists utilized Kava as a diuretic, anesthetic, antispasmodic, aphrodisiac, and sedative. It was used to treat urinary tract infections, asthma, gout, headaches, and arthritis[9][11][14][15]. It is also a known appetite stimulant and aids with neuralgia and genito-urinary inflammation[84].

Psychobotanical Uses: There is growing evidence that Kava is an effective natural remedy for anxiety symptoms[86]. It works as a mild sedative and calmative that can attenuate insomnia, relieve stress, lessen tension, and produce a state of euphoria[3][11]. Kava helps with mood elevation, relaxation, irritability, agitation, restlessness, mental alertness, muscle spasms, and muscle tension[3][9][92]. Some studies have shown that Kava significantly reduces anxiety symptoms within the first week of consumption[14]. Other studies have demonstrated that Kava helps manage moderate to severe generalized anxiety, social phobia, restless leg syndrome, and agoraphobia[3]. One clinical investigation demonstrated that adults who took 200 mg of Kava extract over four weeks showed significant reductions in anxiety and associated sleep problems[57].

Guidance: Kava's dried root is the part used medicinally. It may be consumed in tea or tincture forms. For tea, add 2 tsp dried root to one cup of boiling water. Simmer for 20-30 minutes; allow to sit 10 minutes. Drink 1-3 times daily. For tincture, add 1 part dried bark to 5 parts 65% alcohol (may substitute with vegetable glycerin or apple cider vinegar). Consume 1 tsp as needed. It should not be used for more than three months at a time. Avoid while driving or operating heavy machinery. Prolonged use may alter liver enzymes. Avoid while pregnant or lactating. Avoid if diagnosed with Parkinson's disease. Do not combine with alcohol or other sedatives. Consult with a primary care doctor before use. If using a commercial product, follow the instructions on the package.

Lavender

This aromatic flowering plant has long been celebrated for its fragrance and beauty. Known scientifically as Lavandula angustifolia, lavender is native to the Mediterranean and Northern Africa and belongs to the same family as mint and sage. The word "lavender" comes from the Latin word "lavar," which translates into "to wash" or "purify." It is now cultivated worldwide as a cosmetic, fragrance, flavoring, and medicinal agent.

Historical/Traditional Uses: Early Egyptians used lavender in rituals and rites and for its purifying properties. Medicinally, lavender was used in the 19th century as a digestive aid, sleep aid, insecticide, antiseptic and antimicrobial (for wounds), and analgesic (for headaches and migraines)[6][15]. Due to the pleasantness of its natural aroma, it was also utilized as a "strewing herb" (an herb used to mask bad odors) [1]. African American folk herbalists used lavender to treat insect bites and stings[27].

Psychobotanical Uses: Lavender is a relatively safe herb for people who are high-strung[11], keyed up or on edge, irritable, nervous, and agitated[3][8][9]. It possesses anxiolytic properties[20][48][75] that help calm the mind and body[1][6], alleviate head and muscle tension[11][75], and relieve stress[6][8][10][12][75]. Clinical trials suggest that lavender is an effective treatment for relieving symptoms of generalized anxiety disorder[11]. Other research studies among hospice patients demonstrated that lavender aromatherapy significantly reduced anxiety and pain levels[67]. Lavender aromatherapy helps calm racing thoughts, elevate mood, and achieve 'mindful presence'[92]. Lavender is also useful in managing anxiety-related digestive problems[1], hypertension[75], and insomnia caused by nervous conditions[5][96].

Guidance: Dried and fresh lavender flowers, bark, and oil extract may be used medicinally. For tea, steep 1 tbsp of plant material in 1 cup of hot water for 15-25 minutes. Strain and drink as needed. For tincture, add 1 part dried bark to 5 parts 75% alcohol (may substitute with vegetable glycerin or apple cider vinegar). Consume 1 tsp two times daily. If using a commercial product, follow the instructions on the package.

Lemon Balm

This fragrant herb goes by many names, including Melissa balm, bee balm, sweet balm, honey plant, and English balm. Native to North Africa, the Mediterranean, Europe, and Western Asia, it is highly prized for its medicinal, cosmetic, and culinary properties. Known scientifically as Melissa officinalis (Mint family), Lemon balm is now cultivated worldwide. This low-growing herb can be recognized by its dense bushes of lemon-scented leaves, small two-lipped white flowers, and square stems. The leaves are deeply-veined and toothy.

Historical/Traditional Uses: Folk healers have long employed Lemon balm in the treatment of fevers, painful menses, heart disease, mumps, herpes, headaches, cold sores, insect bites, and a host of other viral and bacterial infections[1][5][10][15]. It is a well-established carminative, antibacterial, antiparasitic, nootropic, antispasmodic, and diaphoretic[3][75][84]. Other traditional uses include its application to hypertension, hyperthyroidism, and gastrointestinal problems[75]. Lemon balm was also utilized as a "strewing herb" due to the pleasantness of its natural aroma[1].

Psychobotanical Uses: Herbalists tout Lemon balm's use as a nerve tonic, mild sedative, and calmative[1]. Reputedly, it calms and soothes the central nervous system[1][10][14], and helps manage the "overwhelmed mind"[12]. Hence, it was often referred to as "the gladdening herb"[8][75]. It can help with panic, nervousness, irritability, restlessness, anxiety-related digestive and gastrointestinal issues, and deficits in attention and concentration[1][3][11][13][15]. It aids in alleviating nervous exhaustion, inducing a sense of calm/peace, quieting the mind, uplifting the spirit, and improving sleep quality[10][12][13]. Folk healers extolled its ability to treat insomnia caused by nervous conditions[5]. Research studies support the use of Lemon balm in the management of chronic anxiety[15], as well as agitation among patients with Alzheimer's disease[11]. People who struggle with depressed mood and Seasonal Affective Disorder may also experience relief from this herb[2][9][10]. Lemon balm is also helpful for people with digestive and cardiac problems stemming from psychosomaticism[11][14] and useful in the treatment of anxiety-induced heart palpitations[75]. Lemon Balm aromatherapy helps relax the body, promote restful sleep, elevate mood, and ease nervousness[92].

Guidance: Lemon balm's dried and fresh aerial parts are used medicinally. It may be consumed in tea or tincture forms. For tea, add 3/4 tsp to one cup of boiling water. Steep for 20 minutes and consume. Drink up to four cups per day. For tincture, add 1 part dried leaves to 5 parts 65% alcohol (may substitute with vegetable glycerin or apple cider vinegar). Consume 1 tsp three times daily. If using a commercial product, follow the instructions on the package. Consult with a primary care doctor before use. Avoid if currently taking thyroid medication.

Lemon Verbena

Known commonly as lemon beebrush, this deciduous shrub grows native to South America (i.e., Chile and Argentina). Botanically named Aloysia triphylla/citriodora, Lemon verbena is a member of the Verbenaceae family of tropical flowering plants. It is recognized by its bright, shiny lance-shaped leaves with glossy topsides and tiny white or lilac flowers.

Historical/Traditional Uses: Lemon verbena has historically been used as an antispasmodic, carminative, sedative, and tonic for digestive and hepatic problems[1][6]. It is valued for its ability to stimulate liver and gall bladder function, soothe digestive discomfort, improve recovery after physical exertion, and reduce fever in children[11][16].

Psychobotanical Uses: Like lemon balm, Lemon verbena emits a fragrant, citrusy scent that many find soothing, restorative, and relaxing[6][11][16]. As a nervine, this herb reputedly "lifts the spirits"[8][11] and helps manage chronic stress, anxiety, and insomnia[6][16]. Aromatherapy with Lemon verbena also helps elevate and uplift mood[92].

Guidance: Lemon verbena's dried aerial parts are used medicinally. For tea, add 1-2 tsp of plant material to 1 cup of hot water and allow to infuse for 15 minutes. Drink daily or as needed. If using a commercial product, follow the instructions on the package.

Linden

This flowering, ornamental, deciduous tree is cultivated and admired worldwide for its stately stature. Also known as the American basswood, it grows throughout the rich woods of Canada and the United States. Linden features heart-shaped leaves with tiny, toothy ridges and a fibrous inner bark that can be pulled away into thin strips (sometimes these are twisted in cords and mats). Known botanically as Tilia Americana, it belongs to the Mallow family.

Historical/Traditional Uses: Linden has a long-standing history of use as a sleep aid, diaphoretic, antispasmodic, diuretic, and sedative[16]. Early healers used it to treat a variety of conditions, ranging from sinus headaches, fevers, colds, and flu to high blood pressure, tuberculosis, and chicken pox[5][6][11][9][16]. Other uses include its treatment of mild pain and inflammation[96].

Psychobotanical Uses: A lesser-known quality of this widely popular tree is its medicinal value. Linden has been recognized as a soothing nervine that relieves stress, alleviates restlessness, and reduces head and muscle tension among anxiety sufferers[8][9]. As a relatively safe and mild sedative, Linden helps relieve stress-induced gastrointestinal problems[92]. It is recommended to people experiencing mild anxiety symptoms and chronic stress in their daily lives. Linden helps calm the mind and spirit, promote relaxation[96], and manage muscle spasms[6][11][92]. It has also reputedly been used to treat anxiety-related heart palpitations and panic, specifically[11].

Guidance: Linden flowers and leaves are used medicinally, though the flowers are said to elicit the best therapeutic effects. For tea, steep leaves, flowers, and buds in 1 cup of water for 10-15 minutes. Consume one cup of tea 1-3 times daily. For tincture, add 1 part plant material to 5 parts 60% alcohol (may substitute with vegetable glycerin or apple cider vinegar). Consume 1 tsp daily as needed. If using a commercial product, follow the instructions on the package.

Magnolia

This highly-regarded evergreen tree produces the most fragrant and beautiful white blooms with broad, ovate leaves. Native to China, Chinese healers have employed this plant for centuries. Botanically known as Magnolia officinalis, this species grows in the mountainous regions and valleys of China and other parts of the world. It belongs to the Magnoliaceae family.

Historical/Traditional Uses: Though widely celebrated for its sweet-scented blossoms, the medicinal value of the tree's bark is of equal importance. Magnolia bark has been used as a carminative, analgesic, digestive aid, and nootropic[11]. It helps with cramping, flatulence, vomiting, and diarrhea. In traditional Chinese medicine, Magnolia bark is used to treat allergies, sleep disorders, and convulsions[75].

Psychobotanical Uses: Herbalists have touted the application of Magnolia bark to psychological symptoms. It is a widely accepted remedy for anxiety, depression, chronic stress, and sleep-related problems[48][75]. Two clinical research studies on a sample of menopausal women demonstrated that Magnolia's bark extract helped elevate mood and relieve anxiety[11]. Another clinical trial showed that Magnolia bark extract significantly reduced stress cortisol levels in a small sample of adult men and women who took 500 mg daily for four weeks[37]. The adults reported improved mood and significant reductions in emotional stress, tension, fatigue, and anger as a result of use. This plant may be helpful to people who experience tension headaches, low mood, memory deficits, and gastrointestinal problems due to anxiety, [8][11][36].

Guidance: Magnolia bark and fruit are used in medicinal remedies. For tea, add 1-2 tsp of plant material to one cup of boiled water. Steep and cover for 20-30 minutes. Drink up to three cups daily. Consult with a primary care doctor before use. Avoid during pregnancy. If using a commercial product, follow the instructions on the package.

Matrimony Vine

This sprawling vine is known by many names, including Wolfberry, Goji, Goji berry, Mede berry, Chinese boxthorn, and red medlar. It is native to Asia, parts of North Africa, and the Middle Eastern region, and has often been used as a hedge shrub in landscaping. Botanically named Lycium barbarum, this deciduous and woody shrub belongs to the Nightshade family. It is recognized by its bright red berries, trumpet-shaped flowers, and long and narrow leaves with thorny stems.

Historical/Traditional Uses: Matrimony vine has been administered in China for thousands of years to treat liver and kidney problems, impotence, and eye disorders[16]. It is also known as a hypotensive, immune stimulant, and blood tonic.

Psychobotanical Uses: Applied to the management of anxiety symptoms, Matrimony vine helps improve sleep quality, heighten mental acuity, promote calmness, and enhance well-being[5].

Guidance: Matrimony vine berries are consumed for medicinal purposes. Fresh and dried berries may be consumed as tincture or added to cereal, yogurt, soups, or stews. Consume up to 1 oz daily. Consult a primary care doctor before use. Avoid use while pregnant. Leaves are toxic when ingested in large amounts. If using a commercial product, follow the instructions on the package.

Mimosa

This ornamental tree is celebrated for its beautiful flowers and fern-like leaves. Known commonly as the 'Persian silk tree,' its flowers resemble thousands of silk threads in rich hues of pink. Known scientifically as Albizia julibrissin (Fabaceae/Legume family), Mimosa is native to Persia but widely cultivated in many parts of the world. It is considered invasive due to its tendency to spread and thrive in various types of soils, rooting itself in open areas, along roadways, and forest edges.

Historical/Traditional Uses: Medicinally, Mimosa's bark and flowers have been utilized as a natural pain killer, memory enhancer, digestive tonic, and sleep aid[5][9].

Psychobotanical Uses: Herbalists have long touted this plant's ability to manage a host of mental health concerns, including irritability[9], poor distress tolerance, stress-induced cognitive difficulties, stress-induced insomnia[2][5][75], and agitation. Mimosa promotes a sense of calm, relaxation, and mindful presence. It may also be helpful for people who struggle with intense sadness or depressed mood[5].

Guidance: Mimosa flowers and bark extract have anxiolytic and antidepressant effects. For flower tea, add 1 tbsp of dried flowers to one cup of freshly boiled water. Cover and let steep for 15-20 minutes. For bark tea, add 2 tbsp of dried bark to two cups of water. Simmer for 20-35 minutes. Consume up to 4 cups daily. For tincture, add 1 part dried bark to 5 parts 50% alcohol (may substitute with vegetable glycerin or apple cider vinegar). If using fresh flowers, add 1 part flowers to 2 parts 50% alcohol (may substitute with vegetable glycerin or apple cider vinegar). Consume 1 tsp up to four times daily. If using a commercial product, follow the instructions on the package. Avoid during pregnancy.

Motherwort

This invasive, perennial wildflower is native to Asia and naturalized in Northern Africa, Europe, and America. Known botanically as Leonurus cardiaca, it features palm-shaped leaves and small pink flowers tightly embedded into prickly stems. It can be found in fields, wastelands, wooded areas, and roadsides. Common names include 'mother's herb,' 'mother's little helper,' lion's tail, heart wort, and lion's heart. It belongs to the Lamiaceae (Mint) family.

Historical/Traditional Uses: Motherwort has been utilized to treat digestive problems, heart conditions, hypertension, hyperthyroidism, neuralgia, sciatica, and women's reproductive issues (i.e., promotes and regulates menstruation, facilitates childbirth, manages premenstrual syndrome and menopausal symptoms)[1][5][8][9][11]. It is valued as an antispasmodic, diuretic, sedative, cardiotonic, immune-stimulant, and antioxidant.

Psychobotanical Uses: As a popular nervine, Motherwort also has a longstanding history of treatment for mental health issues. It is helpful in the management of irritability, mood swings, nervousness, intense sadness, exposure to chronic stress, and panic symptoms[2][3][9]. Additionally, herbalists have lauded its use in the treatment of stress-induced arrhythmia, heart palpitations[3][65], and hypertension[75]. It helps soothe anxiety, agitation, promotes relaxation, and is particularly helpful in treating postpartum mental and physical health concerns (hence the name)[9][11][12][16][92].

Guidance: Motherwort's aerial parts are used medicinally. For tea, add 1 tsp of plant material to one cup of hot water. Let infuse for 10 minutes. Consume one cup 2-3 times daily. For tincture, add 1 part dried leaves to 5 parts 60% alcohol (may substitute with vegetable glycerin or apple cider vinegar). Consume 1 tsp three times daily. Motherwort is bitter, so only those who can tolerate it may consume it in tea form. Consult primary care doctor before use. It may trigger uterine contractions, so avoid use while pregnant. If using a commercial product, follow the instructions on the package.

Mugwort

This flowering perennial goes by many names, including wormwood, Chrysanthemum weed, felon herb, sailor's tobacco, Old Uncle Henry, Naughty man, and St. John's plant. Native to Africa, Asia, and Europe, it has long been cultivated and utilized for medicinal properties. Known scientifically as Artemisia vulgaris (Asteraceae family), this relatively invasive plant can be found growing in wastelands and along roadsides. Mugwort is recognized by its dark green leaves with hairy undersides, red to purple stems, and small yellow flowers that bloom in the summer and fall.

Historical/Traditional Uses: Mugwort is widely known as an antibacterial, diaphoretic, antiseptic, anti-inflammatory, antispasmodic, and digestive tonic. It has been used to treat digestive complaints, respiratory ailments, kidney problems, epilepsy, malaria, and wounds[6]. This plant is rich in antioxidants and valuable as a uterine tonic, diuretic, appetite stimulant, immune booster, and kidney cleanser[96].

Psychobotanical Uses: As a nerve tonic, Mugwort is used to treat psychological and neurological conditions, including anxiety, chronic stress, depression, and epilepsy[71]

[72][96]. Herbalists include Mugwort root in many remedies for irritability, restlessness, and insomnia[89], and its teas help achieve a sense of calm[6].

Guidance: The dried leaves of Mugwort are used medicinally. They may be consumed as tea or smoked. For tea, add 1 tsp of dried leaves to 1 cup hot water, let infuse for 10 minutes. Drink 1-2 cups daily. Avoid while pregnant (potentially an abortifactant). If using a commercial product, follow instructions on the package.

Muira Puama

Native to the Amazonian rainforests of Brazil, this flowering tree has been used extensively by Indigenous peoples. Known botanically as Ptychopetalum olacoides, this plant is recognizable by its tall height (up to fifty feet), dark brown leaves, white flowers, and the orange-ish fruit it bears. It goes by many names, including marapuama, potency wood, and potenzholz. Muira puama belongs to the Olacaceae family.

Historical/Traditional Uses: Muira puama has historically been used as an aphrodisiac[3][96], as well as a treatment for rheumatism, poor circulation, menstrual irregularity, neuromuscular pain, diarrhea, erectile dysfunction, baldness, and mild cases of paralysis[9][11][15]. Other uses include its treatment for gastrointestinal ailments and upper respiratory problems (i.e., bronchitis, coughs, and sore throat)[96].

Psychobotanical Uses: As an adaptogen and nervine, Muira puama aids in the relief of nervous exhaustion, promotes relaxation, diminishes tension, and soothes stress among anxiety sufferers[3][9][46]. It is also considered a neuroprotective tonic[46].

Guidance: Muira puama's tree bark, roots, and leaves are used medicinally. For tincture, add 1 part dried bark to 5 parts 70% alcohol (may substitute with vegetable glycerin or apple cider vinegar). Consume 1/2 tsp every morning. If using a commercial product, follow the instructions on the package.

Northern Prickly Ash

This thorny, deciduous shrub can be found on hillsides, high cliffs, open woodlands, roadsides, and marshes of Canada, as well as in the Northeast and Midwestern regions of the United States. Known commonly as the Toothache tree or Suterberry, it bears compound leaves with toothy leaflets, thorny leafstalks, and twigs (hence the "prickly" part of the name). Botanically named Zanthoxylum americanum, this tree belongs to the Rutaceae family of citrus plants. Not surprisingly, the leaves emit a lemony scent when crushed.

Historical/Traditional Uses: Medicinally, Northern prickly-ash was used to treat rheumatism, kidney problems, cardiac conditions, respiratory ailments, neurological problems, and uterine cramps[5][11]. Plant medicine practitioners promote this herb as a stimulant for the lymphatic and circulatory systems, and a pain-relieving agent[3]. Indigenous peoples of North America traditionally chewed the leaves and twigs to relieve toothaches[5][11][47]. It also helped alleviate arthritis[11]. Enslaved African Americans also used the bark as a blood tonic and remedy for swollen feet[103].

Psychobotanical Uses: A lesser-known benefit of

this plant is the use of its bark for nervousness and stress-induced fatigue. As a stimulating herb, Northern prickly-ash can be used to treat anxiety-related exhaustion and weakness[5].

Guidance: The bark and berries of the Northern prickly-ash are used in medicinal remedies. For tincture, add 1 part dried bark to 5 parts 65% alcohol (may substitute with vegetable glycerin or apple cider vinegar). Consume 1/4 tsp up to 3 times daily. If using a commercial product, follow the instructions on the package.

Passionflower

This climbing perennial vine is native to North, Central, and South America and grows along roadsides and fields. Commonly known as Maypop (due to its tendency to bloom in May), Passionflower produces the most exotic pinkish purple flowers that are said to represent the crucifixion of Christ. It also features egg-shaped orange fruit, and three-lobed, elongated leaves with serrated edges. Scientifically named Passiflora incarnata (Passifloraceae family), this plant has a well-documented history of therapeutic and neuropsychiatric benefits.

Historical/Traditional Uses: Nineteenth-century herbalists touted Passionflower's use as a digestive aid (e.g., for diarrhea), as well as its ability to treat menstrual discomfort, epilepsy, whooping cough, toothaches, and skin wounds[15]. The Mayans utilized its leaves to treat inflammation (as a poultice), while other Indigenous groups found it useful as a blood tonic[16].

Psychobotanical Uses: A well-known nervine and sedative, Passionflower leaves have been used to manage chronic worry[8], rumination and circular thinking[2][75], psychomotor agitation[9], irritability[11], restlessness[5][14], physical tension[3][11], heart palpitations, and stress-induced headaches[9][16]. Evidence shows that early Indigenous Americans, like the Algonquin, utilized it as a tranquilizing herb to calm nervousness[11]. It is a relatively gentle sedative and tranquilizer that can produce a relaxing effect. Reputedly, Passionflower helps manage sleep problems, especially insomnia caused by chronic worry, inability to "turn off thinking," "mental chatter," and nightmares[3][8][9][14][20]. A clinical study among people with Generalized Anxiety Disorder showed significant reductions in anxiety symptoms after four weeks of taking Passionflower in extract form[28]. The study participants reported relief in nervous stress, restlessness, insomnia, and overall anxiety (as measured by the Hamilton Anxiety Rating Scale). The same study demonstrated that Passionflower was just as effective as 30 mg of Oxazepam, a widely used prescription anti-anxiety medication. It contains major bioactive compounds chemically similar to morphine[15].

Guidance: Passionflower is most often consumed in tincture form, though tea using the dried leaves and other aerial parts is helpful. For tea, consume .25-1 g up to 3 times daily. For tincture, add 1 part plant material to 8 parts 45% alcohol (may substitute with vegetable glycerin or apple cider vinegar). Consume 1.5 tsp three times daily. Passionflower may cause drowsiness, so it is best consumed before bedtime. Consult with a primary care doctor before use. Avoid driving or operating heavy machinery after use. Avoid while taking prescription blood thinners. Avoid excessive use while pregnant or nursing. If using a commercial product, follow the instructions on the package.

Peppermint

This popular and widely cultivated perennial herb is packed with high commercial value. It grows abundantly in many parts of the world, including North America, South Africa, Europe, and Australia. As a hybrid of spearmint and watermint plants, Peppermint can be found in a variety of everyday products, ranging from bubblegum to fragrances. It is recognized by its strong aroma, square stems, underground and surface runners, and narrow or egg-shaped veined leaves with sharply serrated edges. Known scientifically as Mentha x piperita, it belongs to the Lamiaceae family.

Historical/Traditional Uses: Peppermint has a longstanding history of use among ancient people. Dried leaves were even found in Egyptian pyramids from 1000 BCE [11][15]. Indigenous American and folk healers have also used peppermint leaves in their treatments for various health concerns. It is a well-known digestive aid, expectorant, analgesic, antispasmodic, and emetic [1]. It can relieve everything from coughs, colds, and fevers to colic, indigestion, nausea, and headaches [3][5][10][11].

Psychobotanical Uses: For anxiety sufferers, Peppermint provides relief for insomnia, relaxes muscles, reduces muscle tension, and mitigates panic attacks (especially when inhaled as aromatherapy or applied to the temples)[3][5]. Aromatherapy with Peppermint helps alleviate stress, rejuvenate the mind, and manage fear[92].

Guidance: Peppermint's fresh and dried leaves may be used medicinally. For tea, add 1 tbsp of dried leaves to 2/3 cup of boiling water and steep for 10-15 minutes. For tincture, add 1 part plant material to 5 parts 50% alcohol (may substitute with vegetable glycerin or apple cider vinegar). Consume 1 tsp three times daily. If using a commercial product, follow the instructions on the package.

Pink Lady's Slipper/Yellow Lady's Slipper

As the name implies, this perennial herb produces flowers with petals that closely resemble a pouch or shoe. Native to North America, Pink lady's slipper and Yellow lady's slipper both commonly grow in forests and woodlands and thrive best in wet, muddy, and acidic soil. Pink lady's slipper features pinkish petals (sometimes white), while Yellow lady's slipper produces striking yellow flowers with purple streaks. The former is botanically named Cypripedium acaule, and commonly named Moccasin flower or American valerian. The botanical name for the latter is Cypripedium parviflorum, commonly referred to as hairy yellow lady's slipper and American valerian. Both flowers belong to the Orchid family and can substitute for one another.

Historical/Traditional Uses: Pink lady's slipper and Yellow lady's slipper were extensively used by the Indigenous people of North America for ailments ranging from labor pains to intestinal worms[5][11]. Nineteenth-century eclectic physicians learned of its medicinal uses from the native healers and began using it as a uterine tonic, aphrodisiac, fever reducer, and treatment for menstrual irregularities. The Gullah Geechee people of South Carolina (descendants of West and Central Africans) also utilized this orchid plant, applying it in the treatment of headaches[82].

Psychobotanical Uses: Both lady's slippers are not just sedatives, but versatile tranquilizing herbs. They have been used to treat a wide range of anxiety and stress-induced symptoms, including tension headaches, heart palpitations, restlessness, panic attacks, muscular tension, and insomnia[5] [11]. Their calming effects are not limited to physical symptoms, but also extend to psychological distress, irritability, agitation, racing thoughts, and over-excitement. As noted by medical herbalist Andrew Chevalier, lady's slipper "reduces emotional tension and often calms the mind sufficiently to allow sleep."[11]

Guidance: Lady's slippers root/rhizomes are used in medicinal remedies. For tea, add 1 tsp of dried plant material per cup of boiled water. Simmer for 20-30 minutes. Consume up to two cups daily. The active ingredients are not water soluble, so tincture may be most effective. If using a commercial product, follow the instructions on the package. Pink and Yellow Lady's Slippers take years to grow, and harvesting the root destroys the entire plant. Do not over-harvest in order to protect this plant species.

Poison Devil's Pepper

C ommonly named 'swizzle stick,' this small perennial tree and shrub is native to the moist forests and tropical savannas of sub-Saharan Africa. Scientifically named Rauwolfia vomitoria (Apocynaceae family), it is recognized by its dark green, elliptical, pointed leaves, fragrant white flowers, and purplish-black fruit.

Historical/Traditional Uses: African herbalists have used Poison devil's pepper for centuries. The plant has been employed to treat smallpox, epilepsy, constipation, indigestion, and malarial fever[59]. Pharmaceutical companies have also exported this plant for its rich source of reserpine (a chemical compound used in hypertension medication).

Psychobotanical Uses: Poison devil's pepper is highly valued for its tranquilizing and sedative properties. Folk healers have used the plant to treat chronic anxiety induced by hypertension, restlessness, and "aggressive maniac behavior"[59]. Small-scale laboratory studies have also demonstrated that root bark extract possesses anxiolytic effects[93].

Guidance: Traditional African remedies involve heating or boiling the root, stem bark, leaves, and fruit for medicinal preparations. If using a commercial extract, follow the instructions on the package. Teas may also be made from the powdered root. For root tea, add 1-3 tsp of powder per one cup of tea. Drink one cup daily, beginning with the lowest dose and increasing gradually. Consult with a primary care doctor before use. The alkaloids are known to cause depression.

Pulsatilla

Also known as the Pasque flower, this perennial wildflower is a member of the Buttercup family and produces a stunning purple (sometimes white) flower with small sepals. Pulsatilla is native to Europe's Central and Northern regions, grows abundantly in many areas of the United States, and is cultivated worldwide. It is the state flower of South Dakota, and can be found in open prairies, meadows, woods, and particularly rocky soils. It is scientifically named Anemone pulsatilla and belongs to the Buttercup family.

Historical/Traditional Uses: Pulsatilla was widely used by the Indigenous peoples of North America and earlier naturopaths. It was used to treat various conditions, ranging from rheumatism, respiratory problems, and toothaches to eye ailments, skin conditions, and menstrual problems[5][11][84].

Psychobotanical Uses: Pulsatilla is recognized as a powerful nervine that treats a host of anxiety-related symptoms, including nervousness, agitation, distress, over-excitability, intense phobic reactions, chronic worry, tension headaches, nervous exhaustion, and stress-induced insomnia[9][11][75]. Medical ethnobotanist Huron Smith described it as the "treatment of choice" for melancholia in 1933[18]. Late 19th-century eclectic physicians touted its ability to manage "nervousness and despondency," "unnatural fear," "tendency to weep," and "morbid mental excitement," among other symptoms[84]. It has also been indicated in the treatment of anxiety in young pubescent girls[75].

Guidance: Pulsatilla's dried aerial parts are utilized for their therapeutic benefits, preferably in tincture or extract form. The fresh plant is recognized as toxic. For tincture, add 1 part dried plant material to 5 parts 50% alcohol (may substitute with vegetable glycerin or apple cider vinegar). Consume 1 to 3 drops daily in diluted water. If using a commercial product, follow the instructions on the package.

Rhodiola

This hardy, resilient, cold-weather perennial plant grows in the extreme environments of Canada, Alaska, Asia, Scandinavia, and Siberia. Its clusters of yellow flowers with thick, oblong leaves can be found along mountains and cliffs and grow mainly in the wild. Commonly named golden root, rose root, and arctic root, it belongs to the Crassulaceae family (a diverse group of succulents).

Historical/Traditional Uses: Botanically referred to as Rhodiola rosea, this plant was traditionally used to improve fertility and treat colds, flu, and other respiratory infections. However, it has historically been revered for its adaptogenic properties. Rhodiola is celebrated as a full-body tonic that improves endurance and stamina, boosts energy while decreasing fatigue, enhances mental and physical performance, and quickens recovery from psychological and physical challenges[8][11][75]. Research studies on Rhodiola use among Russian athletes, military and cosmonauts demonstrated its performance-enhancing capabilities[13][75]. Other uses include its application to altitude sickness, ischemic heart disease, and angina pectoris[75].

Psychobotanical Uses: Rhodiola has a proven track record in managing a wide range of anxiety and stress symptoms[8], particularly those related to cognitive impairments. It aids anxiety sufferers in maintaining mental clarity, enhancing memory, recovering from mental fatigue, reducing stress levels, and safeguarding against the long-term effects of chronic stress[13]. A small, randomized clinical study of Rhodiola revealed that it significantly alleviated anxiety symptoms in participants who took a dose of extract in the morning and before lunch for fourteen days[31]. Furthermore, small-scale studies have suggested that Rhodiola could be as effective as prescription medications for Generalized Anxiety Disorder[8][43]. A lesser known benefit is its ability to treat anxiety induced by nicotine withdrawal[75].

Guidance: Rhodiola's dried and fresh rhizomes are the parts used medicinally. In tea form, drink 1-2 cups daily. For tincture, add 1 part dried plant material to 5 parts 50% alcohol (may substitute with vegetable glycerin or apple cider vinegar). Consume 1.5 tsp three times daily. Rhodiola may exacerbate sleep problems, increase irritability, and is not advisable for those diagnosed with bipolar disorders[9][11]. If using a commercial product, follow the instructions on the package. Consult with a primary care doctor or psychiatrist before use.

Rosemary

This aromatic, evergreen perennial shrub, scientifically known as Salvia rosmarinus, is a star player in the culinary world. Native to the Mediterranean region, Rosemary is characterized by its needle-like leaves that give off a distinct aroma when crushed, and its pale blue to blue-violet flowers that bloom in the spring and summer. Rosemary belongs to the Lamiaceae (Mint) family.

Historical/Traditional Uses: Medicinally, Rosemary has a longstanding history in folk medicine and herbal traditions. It is a celebrated antioxidant, expectorant, antiseptic, antispasmodic, and carminative agent. Among its many uses, it has been employed in the treatment of rheumatism[1], headaches[10][16], respiratory conditions[15], memory and concentration difficulty[1][15][16], circulatory issues[3], and digestive problems[3][9]. Other minor applications include its uses for baldness, dandruff, and bad breath[15].

Psychobotanical Uses: As a nervine, Rosemary is not just a cerebral tonic, but a reliable one that ensures vitality and promotes well-being. It is particularly effective for anxiety and anxious debility, stress-induced cognitive deficits, and chronic stress[2]. Its calming properties help soothe nervous agitation, promote sleep quality, and enhance cognitive performance[1][2][32][92].

Guidance: Rosemary's dried and fresh leaves, as well as extracts, are used medicinally. It may be consumed as a tea, tincture, or an edible herb. For tea, add 2 tsp to one cup of boiling water. Simmer for 15-20 minutes and strain. Drink up to four times daily. For tincture, add 1 part dried leaves to 5 parts 65% alcohol (may substitute with vegetable glycerin or apple cider vinegar). Consume 1/2 tsp up to three times daily. If using a commercial product, follow the instructions on the package. Consult with a primary care doctor before use, especially if taking hypertension medications, diuretics, or anticoagulants[2].

Sacred Lotus

This aquatic perennial plant is revered and celebrated among Hindus and Buddhists. Known botanically as Nelumbo nucifera, it is recognizable by its large, beautiful, and fragrant flowers, paper-thin petals, and broad umbrella-like leaves that float gently on the surface of water. The Sacred Lotus thrives in ponds, lakes, ditches, and other slow-moving bodies of water. It belongs to the Nelumbonaceae family.

Historical/Traditional Uses: The Sacred Lotus has a longstanding history of use among Buddhists and Hindus. Medicinally, it has been utilized to treat a host of conditions, ranging from diarrhea and premature ejaculation to liver and immune system issues[5].

Psychobotanical Uses: The Sacred Lotus is recommended for a host of anxiety-related symptoms, including restlessness, agitation, insomnia, and heart palpitations. An exploratory study of the Sacred Lotus showed that adults who took an oral daily dose of 1,000 mg of leaf extract (500 mg twice daily) experienced significant reductions in anxiety after twenty-eight days[68]. These findings support earlier animal studies that demonstrated significant anxiolytic activity in study subjects, comparable to diazepam[69][70].

Guidance: The entire lotus plant has historically been used medicinally. For anxiety, the leaves and cotyledons from sprouting seeds may be eaten or brewed in tea remedies. For tea, add 1-2 tsp of plant material to one cup of boiled water. Steep and cover for 15-20 minutes. Drink up to three cups daily. If using a commercial product, follow the instructions on the package.

Sceletium

B otanically named Mesembryanthemum tortuosum, this perennial succulent herb is commonly found in the western and northern cape provinces of South Africa. It goes by many names, including kanna, channa, or kougoed, and has been used by the San and Khoi people since ancient times. Sceletium is recognized by its white and pale yellow flowers (sometimes pink), imbricate leaves with curled tips, and calyx that bear four to five sepals. This medicinal plant belongs to the Aizoaceae family.

Historical/Traditional Uses: Sceletium has been traditionally used as a masticatory, sedative, appetite suppressant, soporific, and analgesic[56][59]. It has been used to treat abdominal pains, toothache, fatigue, and manage hunger/thirst. In addition to its medicinal and social uses, traditional healers utilized Sceletium for spiritual purposes[73].

Psychobotanical Uses: Scientific research studies have noted Sceletium's potential benefits as a natural anxiolytic and antidepressant[56]. Alkaloids from the plant are shown to enhance mood, increase sociability, induce calm and relaxation, relieve stress, reduce tension, and promote general well-being[73]. A double-blind clinical study, a gold standard in scientific research, revealed that adults given a single 25 mg dose of Sceletium extract had significant reductions in subjective anxiety levels (during a simulated public speaking task) [74].

Guidance: Sceletium's dried and fresh plant material may be chewed or consumed in tea or tincture form. For tea, add 1 tsp dried leaves to 1.5 cups of freshly boiling water. Cover and steep for 15-25 minutes. Drink up to two cups daily. Consult with a primary care doctor before use.

Schisandra

This perennial and woody plant is commonly called Chinese magnolia vine and botanically named Schisandra chinensis. It grows native to Northeastern China and Japan and is recognizable by its clusters of bold red berries, pointed egg-shaped leaves, and pink flowers. Schisandra belongs to the diverse family of flowering plants called Schisandraceae.

Historical/Traditional Uses: Schisandra has a rich and enduring history of use in traditional Chinese herbal medicine. It has been a trusted remedy for liver diseases, respiratory infections, memory problems, skin conditions, and sexual difficulties[3][11][15][43]. As an adaptogen and general tonic, it is renowned for its ability to "balance body functions, improve mental function, increase stamina and physical performance, normalize blood sugar and blood pressure, reduce high cholesterol, improve the health of adrenal glands, and energize RNA and DNA molecules to rebuild cells"[3].

Psychobotanical Uses: Schisandra's calming effects make it worthwhile for anxiety sufferers. The berries are said to "quiet the spirit and calm the heart"[11] and relieve emotional tension and stress. Scientific studies have shown that they can reduce insomnia and irritability, treat heart palpitations due to stress, and improve mental function, memory, and attention[3][15][43]. Moreover, Schisandra increases physical stamina, endurance, and coordination, as demonstrated in research studies on its use among Russian athletes, military personnel, and cosmonauts[13]. Previous laboratory studies have also demonstrated the significant anxiolytic effect of a Schisandra lignans extract[100].

Guidance: Schisandra berries, the key medicinal component, offer a variety of consumption methods. They can be chewed or consumed in tea, tincture, capsule, and tonic wine. For tea, add 2 tbsp of dried berries to two cups of boiling water and simmer for 20 minutes. Drink 4-8 ounces three times daily. For tincture, add 1 part dried berries to 3 parts 40% alcohol (may substitute with vegetable glycerin or apple cider vinegar). Consume 1 tsp up to three times daily.

Skullcap

K nown scientifically as Scutellaria lateriflora (Mint family), this wild flowering plant grows abundantly throughout the hedges, wetlands, and riverbanks of the United States and Canada. Hoodwort, helmet flower, mad dog weed, and mad dog skullcap are among its many names. It garnered the name "mad dog" due to its historical reputation as a treatment for rabies bites, a fascinating aspect of its history[18]. The "skullcap" portion of the name was simply due to the resemblance of its dried seed husks to the top part of the human skull.

Historical/Traditional Uses: Skullcap has been employed to treat digestive problems, fibromyalgia, post-stroke paralysis, atherosclerosis, hyperlipidemia, allergies, skin conditions and inflammation[83]. It is also valued as a treatment for menstrual cramps, alcohol withdrawal, migraines, and an overactive libido[96].

Psychobotanical Uses: Folk healers have long relied on this mild sedative to relieve muscle tension, spasms, and nervousness[75][79]. Skullcap has also been shown to treat anxious mood[5][15], panic symptoms[2], rage/angry

150

outbursts[92], agitation due to overstimulation, irritability[15], excitability[16], insomnia[15][92], and stress-induced deficits in attention. A clinical trial on adult subjects demonstrated that 200-350 mg capsules of Skullcap reduced subjective anxiety scores within two hours of consumption. As a powerful and restorative nervine, its calming properties help ease people who feel overwhelmed, chronically frustrated, and lack overall mood stability[12]. Early 20th-century doctors often prescribed it for the treatment of "nervous conditions" due to its tranquilizing effects[15][18]. Other healers used it to treat "hysteria" and muscle tension caused by chronic stress and worry[11]. A 2010 survey conducted among herbal practitioners found that 84% specifically used Skullcap for the treatment of anxiety and stress relief[83]. It may also be used to to manage nervous tension and associated headaches[16][96].

Guidance: The aerial parts of Skullcap are used in medicinal infusions and tinctures. For tea, add 2-3 tsp of dried herb to 16-24 ounces of freshly boiling water. Let steep for 15-20 minutes. Consume up to 3 cups per day. For tincture, add 1 part plant material to 8 parts 25% alcohol (may substitute with vegetable glycerin or apple cider vinegar). Consume 1 tsp four times daily. Avoid use while pregnant or nursing. Skullcap has been indicated in a number of cases involving hepatoxicity. Consult with a primary care doctor before use. If using a commercial product, follow the instructions on the package. Scutellaria lateriflora may be confused with Pink Skullcap (aliases Woodsage), which is toxic.

Skunk Cabbage

As the name implies, this perennial herb emits a pungent, putrid odor resembling rotting meat. Scientifically named Symplocarpus foetidus (Araceae family), it is cultivated worldwide and native to North America's wet, rich woods. Skunk cabbage is identifiable by its tiny purple flowers and cabbage-like leaves and thrives in swamps, marshes, meadows, and bogs' edges.

Historical/Traditional Uses: Skunk cabbage has a longstanding history of use among the Chippewa, Winnebago, Dakota, and Micmac peoples of North America. As a powerful expectorant, it was used to treat asthma, bronchitis, whooping cough, nasal congestion, allergies, and other respiratory conditions[11]. Skunk cabbage was also relied on for its antispasmodic properties in the treatment of muscle spasms and cramps. Its root was also used to treat wounds, inflammation, and headaches.

Psychobotanical Uses: Skunk cabbage's versatility is truly remarkable. Herbalists have discovered its effectiveness in treating a diverse range of conditions, from nervousness and chest pressure to irritability and muscle tension[9].

Guidance: For those interested in harnessing the medicinal benefits of skunk cabbage, the roots and rhizomes are the key components. For tincture, add 1 part dried plant material to 5 parts 50% alcohol (may substitute with vegetable glycerin or apple cider vinegar). Consume 1/4 tsp, diluted in water, up to three times daily. If using a commercial product, follow the instructions on the package.

Spearmint

This renowned perennial herb goes by many names, including common mint, lamb mint, garden mint, and curly mint. As the 'mother of all mints', it is widely celebrated for its culinary, cosmetic, and medicinal value. Scientifically named Mentha spicata (Lamiaceae family), Spearmint can be identified by its light green and wrinkled leaves, square stems, underground runners, and small pink or white flowers. Spearmint is recognized as being sweeter and milder than its peppermint descendent.

Historical/Traditional Uses: Spearmint has been used as a digestive aid and to treat nausea[6] and fevers[15]. It has long been used as both a stimulant and relaxant and is included in remedies to improve nervous system functioning[10].

Psychobotanical Uses: Herbalists have long included Spearmint in herbal remedies for mental health. In the treatment of anxiety, Spearmint is touted for its calming and relaxation effects, ability to reduce muscle tension, and ability to renew energy[10]. Recent animal studies demonstrated the anxiolytic effects of spearmint extract[75].

Guidance: Spearmint leaves and flowers are used in herbal concoctions. For tea, add 2 tbsp of plant material per cup of boiling water. Steep for 20-25 minutes. Drink as needed. If using a commercial product, follow the instructions on the package.

St. John's Wort

This highly-regarded ornamental plant is used extensively for its medicinal properties. Native to Asia and Europe, St. John's Wort produces five-petaled, yellow, star-shaped flowers that bloom at the summer solstice. The timing of its bloom period is around the birthday of the biblical John the Baptist, hence the name, St. John's Wort. Scientifically named Hypericum perforatum, this flowering plant belongs to the Hypericeae family and grows along prairies and meadows. A unique feature of St. John's Wort (and a way to confirm its identity) is the red dye-like sap it produces when crushed. The unique black dots and pinpricks on the underside of the leaves may also distinguish the plant. St. John's Wort is also commonly called St. Joan's Wort, goatweed, and tipton weed.

Historical/Traditional Uses: St. John's Wort has been used both orally and externally to treat severe skin conditions, including ulcers, burns, wounds, sores, snake bites, eczema, and bruises[2][5][14][15][75]. Herbalists have also administered this herb to treat intestinal parasites, diarrhea, bladder problems, herpes, shingles, joint inflammation, and mononu-cleosis[9][10][15].

Psychobotanical Uses: St. John's Wort is widely cele-brated for its nervine properties, including its uses in the treat-ment of mild to moderate depressive symptoms[5][9][11][14] and mania[82]. An added feature is its ability to ameliorate anxiety-induced insomnia, anxious mood, irritability, fearfulness, rest-lessness, and chronic worry[2][9][10][17]. It is often described as a "natural Prozac," as well as a natural monoamine oxidase inhibitor (MAO)[3]. Although the underlying mechanism remains unknown, St. John's Wort has been shown to enhance mood by preventing serotonin reuptake[3]. It may also help manage Seasonal Affective Disorder[10][11], as well as anxi-ety/mood changes induced by menopause or premenstrual syndrome[2][11][16]. Clinical studies among patients with mild to moderate depression showed that St. John's Wort was just as effective as several antidepressants on the market and with fewer side effects. Of note, St. John's Wort counteracts many antidepressant medications and renders them ineffective. Consult with a primary care doctor before use.

Guidance: The flowering tops of St. John's Wort are used medicinally. For tea, add 6 tsp dried plant material per one cup of boiling water. Steep for 10 minutes. Strain and drink 1-4 cups per day. For tincture, add 1 part fresh flowers to 2 parts 95% alcohol (may substitute with vegetable glycerin or apple cider vinegar). Consume 1 tsp three times daily. It may take 2-3 months to achieve noticeable effects. Avoid while taking birth control, antidepressants, anxiolytics, antibi-otics, or blood thinner medications. Consult with a primary care doctor before use. If using a commercial extract, follow the instructions on the package.

Stinging Nettle

Commonly referred to as nettle, nettle leaf, and California nettle, this herbaceous perennial grows freely throughout North America, Africa, Europe, and Asia. Known botanically as Urtica dioica, it can be identified by its prickly and lance-shaped leaves, hairy stems, green flowers, and yellow stamens. It belongs to the Urticaceae family and grows along the edges of woods and fields.

Historical/Traditional Uses: Stinging nettle is a widely celebrated diuretic, anti-inflammatory, antihistamine, astringent, hypotensive, and nutritive tonic. Its leaves are rich in minerals and "help build healthy blood, bones, joints, and skin."[9]. Historically, this plant was used to treat respiratory and arthritic conditions and is particularly helpful in the treatment of anemia, rheumatism, gout, seasonal allergies, tuberculosis, asthma, urinary tract infections, enlarged prostate, insect bites, and wounds[3][5][9][11][96]. Stinging nettle also promotes lactation in nursing mothers[16].

Psychobotanical Uses: In treating anxiety, herbalists utilize Stinging nettle as a relaxant to calm the nervous system[101]. It can help reduce muscle spasms and tension[14] and treat insomnia[82][91]. Laboratory studies have demonstrated its ability to treat diabetes-induced anxiety[102] and memory problems[75]. More research is needed to support its safety and efficacy in the treatment of anxiety.

Guidance: Stinging nettle's leaves, seeds, and roots are used for medicinal remedies. Leaves can be safely eaten (as soup) or consumed as tea or tincture. For tea, add 1 tsp dried leaves per one cup of boiling water. Steep for 15 minutes. Strain and drink 1-4 cups per day. For tincture, add 1 part dried leaves to 4 parts 50% alcohol (may substitute with vegetable glycerin or apple cider vinegar). Consume 1 tsp three times daily. If using a commercial product, follow the instructions on the package. Consult with a primary care doctor before use.

Sweet Everlasting

Also known as Rabbit tobacco, this sweet-smelling herb is widely known for its small white flowers and mild sedating effects. Botanically named Pseudognaphalium obtusifolium, Sweet Everlasting belongs to the Asteraceae family of flowering plants. It grows throughout the Eastern region of the United States and can be found along forest edges, fields, meadows, wooded areas, and roadsides with dry soil.

Historical/Traditional Uses: Sweet Everlasting was used by the Indigenous Americans and African-American folk healers to treat a plethora of respiratory conditions including, asthma, pneumonia, bronchitis, whooping coughs, sore throat, colds, and flu[82][103]. It was also employed to manage digestive complaints (i.e., diarrhea, abdominal cramps, and upset stomach), mumps, and menstrual cramps.

Psychobotanical Uses: There is minimal research on the psychotherapeutic benefits of Sweet Everlasting. However, folk healers and herbalists have long touted its ability to relieve stress, lower anxiety, and lessen muscle tension. It is a mild relaxant and calmative agent with sedating qualities.

Guidance: The leaves and flowers of Sweet Everlasting are often chewed, smoked, or brewed as a tea to access its therapeutic effects. For tea, add 2 tsp of plant material per cup of boiling water. Steep for 10-15 minutes. Drink 1-2 cups as needed. Consult with a primary care doctor before use.

Sweet Marjoram

Known scientifically as Origanum majorana, this aromatic perennial herb is native to the Mediterranean and belongs to the Lamiaceae (Mint) family. Sweet marjoram resembles its cousin oregano and can be recognized by its small, ovate, and hairy leaves with tiny pinkish-white flowers.

Historical/Traditional Uses: Sweet marjoram has been widely used to treat respiratory, gastrointestinal, circulatory, reproductive, and neurological problems[6][88][11]. It is valued medicinally for its antispasmodic, carminative, anti-inflammatory, and stimulant properties[11]. Small-scale studies have also demonstrated its effectiveness in treating polycystic ovary syndrome and vaginitis.

Psychobotanical Uses: A recent study showed that inhalation of Sweet marjoram essential oils (i.e., aromatherapy) effectively reduced anxiety and stress levels among nurses in an intensive care unit[88]. Animal studies have also demonstrated its effectiveness in reducing insomnia associated with anxiety. Anxiety sufferers will also find that Sweet marjoram relieves anxiety mood, improves sleep, and reduces stress levels[6][11][92].

Guidance: Sweet marjoram's dried aerial parts are used medicinally. For tea, add 3 tsp of plant material per cup of boiling water. Steep for 10-15 minutes. Drink 1-2 cups as needed. For tincture, add 1 part plant material to 5 parts 45% alcohol (may substitute with vegetable glycerin or apple cider vinegar). Consume 1 tsp daily as needed. Avoid use while pregnant. If using a commercial product, follow the instructions on the package.

Tall Blue Lettuce

B otanically named Lactuca canadensis, this North American wild lettuce species can be found throughout the United States, Canada, and Alaska. Tall blue lettuce belongs to the Lamiaceae (Mint) family and grows in thickets, along roadsides and woodlands, and in moist open areas. this plant goes by the names, including Canada wild lettuce, Florida blue lettuce, and arrow-leaved lettuce. It is identifiable by its arrow-shaped leaves, milky sap, and yellow dandelion-like flowers.

Historical/Traditional Uses: Tall blue lettuce has been utilized as a natural digestive aid, muscle relaxant, diuretic, and mild pain reliever. It can treat eye conditions, kidney problems, and orthopedic diseases[77], and the milky latex has been used to treat warts, acne, rashes, and other skin ailments[5].

Psychobotanical Uses: Tall blue lettuce can be administered as a mild sedative and nerve tonic for anxiety sufferers. Herbalists tout its mild hypnotic and relaxing effects, more specifically, its ability to ameliorate restlessness, tension, and sleep problems.

Guidance: It is important to note that Tall blue lettuce may be toxic or cause dermatitis. Use with caution and consult with a primary care doctor before use. The leaves and stems are used in medicinal remedies. They are consumed raw or cooked; and may be brewed into tea or prepared as tincture. For tincture, add 1 part fresh plant material (chopped and blended) to 2 parts 95% alcohol (may substitute with vegetable glycerin or apple cider vinegar). Consume 1/2 tsp daily as needed. If using a commercial product, follow instructions on the package.

Thyme

Thyme is a popular culinary herb with a longstanding history. Known botanically as Thymus vulgaris (Lamiaceae Family) and native to the Mediterranean, it is a perennial shrub identifiable by its tiny ovate leaves, woody stems, purple or pink flowers, and strong fragrance.

Historical/Traditional Uses: Thyme's use in the medicinal world is not a recent trend. It has been valued as an expectorant, antibacterial, antifungal, and antimicrobial herb[96]. Thyme is a trusted remedy for respiratory ailments (i.e., asthma, bronchitis, allergies, emphysema, colds, flu, and coughs)[1][2][3][11][16], skin issues[16], digestive problems[3][15], chronic heart conditions[5], urinary tract infections[6][9], and viruses[5][6]. It is also believed to promote menstruation[15] and possess anti-aging properties[11].

Psychobotanical Uses: When applied to mental health, folk healers traditionally used dried Thyme leaves to treat nervousness, low energy, and bodily tension. It is a mood-enhancing herb that promotes sleep quality, tolerance to stress[3], and mental strength[2].

Guidance: Thyme's dried and fresh leaves, as well as

essential oils, can be used in various preparations. For tea, steep 2 tbsp of dried leaves in 1 cup of boiling water. Strain and drink up to four times per day. For tincture, add 1 part plant material to 5 parts 45% alcohol (may substitute with vegetable glycerin or apple cider vinegar). Consume 1.5 tsp three times daily. When using Thyme in herbal remedies, it's important to follow a few safety precautions. Consult with a primary care doctor before use, especially while pregnant. Avoid use if diagnosed with hypertension or epilepsy. If using a commercial product, follow the instructions on the package for a safe and effective experience.

Tiger Lily

This beautiful flower is easily recognized by its orange color and the black, tiger-like spots that adorn each petal. A member of the Liliaceae family, it is known botanically as Lilium lancifolium and commonly known as Devil lily, Leopard lily, and Japanese lily. Tiger lily is native to Eurasia and cultivated worldwide for ornamental gardens.

Historical/Traditional Uses: Tiger lily has long been employed to support female reproductive health and menopause-induced depression[8].

Psychobotanical Uses: A lesser-known quality of this herb is its utilization as a mild sedative. Tiger lily, with its natural and gentle properties, can help ease irritability, relieve stress, and calm anxiety[8]. Ancient Chinese herbal texts have noted the benefits of Tiger lily bulbs in the treatment of anxiety, depression, insomnia, and other "emotional diseases"[78].

Guidance: Tiger lily bulbs may be soaked and consumed raw or cooked. Flower buds are crunchy, sweet, and starchy in texture, resembling the taste of turnips. Tiger lily may also be brewed into tea. If using a commercial product, follow the instructions on the package.

. . .

Twinleaf

K nown commonly as Rheumatism root, Twinleaf is a perennial herb that grows throughout the Eastern region of the United States. Known botanically as Jeffersonia diphylla (Barberry family), it is recognized by its frail white flowers and smooth leaves that resemble butterfly wings. Twinleaf grows and thrives in forests and woodlands near rivers.

Historical/Traditional Uses: Twinleaf has conventionally been used as a diuretic, expectorant, anodyne, and antispasmodic. It treats chronic rheumatism, nerve pain, headaches, urinary tract infections, diarrhea, kidney stones, and skin conditions.

Psychobotanical Uses: Nineteenth-century American herbalists administered Twinleaf to manage "nervous excitability"[84]. Folk herbalists have also used it to treat anxiety symptoms, including muscle and head tension, chronic stress, and stress-induced headaches.

Guidance: Twinleaf's root is utilized in medicinal remedies. For decoction, add 1 tsp of root to one cup of boiling water and steep for 30 minutes. Let simmer for 10 minutes, strain, and consume. For tincture, add 1 part plant material to 5 parts 45% alcohol (may substitute with vegetable glycerin or apple cider vinegar). Consume 1/2 tsp per day. If using a commercial product, follow the instructions on the package. This herb is potentially toxic. Consult a primary care doctor before use and handle with caution.

Valerian

V alerian root has a rich history dating back to ancient
times. Celebrated for its calmative effects, it has been
known by various names such as 'all-heal' and 'garden
heliotrope '. Belonging to the Honeysuckle family, it boasts
over 200 species worldwide. Botanically known as Valeriana
officinalis, this tall, flowering perennial can be spotted in
meadows and grasslands of North America. It is distinguished
by its dark green, pointy leaves and small, pale-pink flowers
that bloom in summer. Its roots and rhizomes, harvested in the
fall, emit an unpleasant odor.

Historical/Traditional Uses: Valerian is a versatile
herb with a multitude of uses. It is widely recognized as a
natural sleep aid, hypnotic, tranquilizer, antispasmodic, sedative, hepato-protectant, diuretic, and nerve tonic. Its traditional use spans a wide range of conditions and ailments, from
mild pain and epilepsy to wound care, intestinal cramps, and
chest congestion.

Psychobotanical Uses: As a potent nervine and mild
sedative, Valerian possesses strong anxiolytic (and non-addictive) properties. It can help ease anxiety, nervous tension[16]

[75], insomnia (i.e., both induce sleep and improve sleep quality)[3][14][92], chronic stress, excitability, mental overactivity, and panic [3][5][8][11][48]. Anxiety sufferers who experience agitation, restlessness, tremors, excessive sweating (not due to heat), muscle tension, panic attacks, and panic-induced heart palpitations may find it helpful in ameliorating symptoms [5][9] [10][13][17]. Valerian is also helpful in the treatment of anxiety-induced digestive problems[8], hypertension, and heart palpitations[16][75]. Touted as an "herbal valium," it can be a great herb for people who have trouble quieting their minds and bodies. According to Dr. Jill Stansbury, a naturopath, Valerian is "probably more helpful in anxiety states than it is for depression"[75]. The late Dr. Sebi, a Honduran herbalist, also noted that Valerian is great for calming and relaxing "frazzled nerves"[6], muscles, and mind"[12]. A small clinical study on patients with Generalized Anxiety Disorder (GAD) showed that a daily dose of Valerian was comparable to taking diazepam (as measured by the Hamilton Anxiety Scale)([13]).

Guidance: Valerian's fresh root and rhizomes are used for medicinal purposes. It may be consumed as root tea, tincture, or extract. For tea, add 1/2 tsp of dried plant material to one cup of boiling water. Steep and consume 4-8 ounces in the evening. For tincture, add 1 part plant material to 5 parts 70% alcohol (may substitute with vegetable glycerin or apple cider vinegar). Consume 1 tsp three times daily. Due to its unpleasant taste, many prefer to consume Valerian as tincture. The maximum benefit of Valerian is typically achieved after two weeks of consumption. Avoid while pregnant or lactating. Do not consume before driving or operating heavy machinery. If using a commercial product, follow the instructions on the package.

Viper's Bugloss

This summer-blooming wildflower, with its violet-blue and purple petals, attracts ample pollinators, especially honeybees. Due to its unusual appearance (and hairy-like bristles), Viper's bugloss is commonly called blueweed, blue thistle, blue devil, Viper's grass, snake flower, and Viper's herb. Known scientifically as Echium vulgare, this plant generally grows along quarries, walls, cliffs, deep gravel pits, and other waste spaces. It can also be found in low-lying coastal regions. It belongs to the Boraginaceae family.

Historical/Traditional Uses: Viper's bugloss is conventionally used as a diuretic, expectorant, diaphoretic, analgesic, and fever reducer[5][11]. It also possesses properties that promote wound healing.

Psychobotanical Uses: While there is limited information and research on the psychotherapeutic benefits of Viper's bugloss, herbalists have found it beneficial in the treatment of nervous complaints, including stress and nervous tension. The use of Viper's bugloss has fallen out of favor due to its toxicity.

Guidance: Viper's bugloss leaves are consumed for

medicinal remedies. For tea, add 1 tsp dried mature leaves to one cup of boiling water. Steep 15-20 minutes. Drink 1-2 cups daily. Consult with a primary care doctor before use, as Viper's bugloss contains highly toxic alkaloids that may be damaging to the liver. It should be handled with caution. If using a commercial product, always follow the instructions on the package.

Virgin's Bower

Virgin's bower is a distinctive climbing vine that can be spotted draping over fences, walls, and other structures in the Southeastern region of the United States. Scientifically known as Clematis virginiana, it belongs to the Buttercup family. Its unique features include abundant clusters of small white flowers, serrated leaves, and woody bases. During the blooming season, Virgin's bower becomes a hub for bees, butterflies, hummingbirds, and other pollinators.

Historical/Traditional Uses: Medicinally, Virgin's bower has been employed to treat various skin conditions, including sores, cuts, chronic itch, and venereal eruptions[79]. The Iroquois of North America relied on this herb to treat kidney and digestive problems.

Psychobotanical Uses: While there is limited information on the anxiolytic properties of VIrgin's bower, early Indigenous healers found it useful in treating sleep problems, nervousness, stress-induced migraines, and muscle tension[5].

Guidance: For those interested in incorporating Virgin's bower into their herbal remedies, it is important to follow the right preparation and usage methods. The roots and leaves of

179

this plant are typically used. For tea, add 1 tsp of the plant material to one cup of freshly boiled water. Steep for 15-25 minutes and drink up to 3 cups daily. Consult with a primary doctor before use, as Virgin's bower is considered highly toxic and should be handled with caution.

Wild Cherry/Black Cherry

This deciduous, woody tree or shrub is widely known as Black cherry, Mountain black cherry, or Rum cherry. It can be found in the Eastern regions of North America and is known botanically as Prunus serotina (Rose family). Wild Cherry is recognized by its dark, purplish fruit, white flowers, and dark green, sharp, and elongated leaves.

Historical/Traditional Uses: Wild cherry has a longstanding history of use as a natural remedy for respiratory and digestive conditions[9][11][82]. As an expectorant, astringent, and febrifuge, the Indigenous Americans relied on it to treat coughs, fevers, laryngitis, bronchitis, pneumonia, diarrhea, hemorrhoids, ulcers, headaches, and many other ailments[5]. Enslaved African Americans on South Carolina plantations used the bark as a blood tonic and remedy for colds[103]. The Gullah Geechee people used Wild cherry to relieve arthritic pain[82] while the Cherokee women used it to manage labor pains[11].

Psychobotanical Uses: Wild cherry contains many active compounds in its inner bark and fruit. It has been touted for its anxiolytic properties, including its ability to treat irritability, restlessness, agitation, nervousness, insomnia, heart palpitations, and muscle tension[5][9].

Guidance: Wild cherry's inner bark and fruit are used in medicinal remedies. For tea, add 1 tsp dried bark per one cup of boiling water. Boil 20-30 minutes, then let stand for 10 minutes. Drink up to 3 cups daily. For tincture, add 1 part fresh bark to 3 parts 40% alcohol (may substitute with vegetable glycerin or apple cider vinegar). Consume 1/4 tsp up to four times daily. While the fruit is edible, the seeds contain compounds that can be toxic in excess. Consult with a primary care doctor before use.

Wild Lettuce

B otanically named Lactuca virosa (Asteraceae family), this biennial herb is commonly found along open prairies, roadsides, riverbanks, and wastelands. Wild lettuce commonly grows throughout the Northern hemisphere and other regions of the world. This herb is characterized by its low-growing, green, spiny leaves, tall dandelion-like yellow flowers, and white milky latex.

Historical/Traditional Uses: Commonly called 'poor man's opium', Wild lettuce is widely known for its sedating analgesic effects. It is traditionally used as a safe relaxant, sleep aid, and cough suppressant[11].

Psychobotanical Uses: As a mild sedative, Wild lettuce has been used to treat insomnia and anxiety. Herbalists tout its ability to promote sleep, relieve muscle tension and spasms[92], and manage nervous agitation, restlessness, and excitability[11]. Dr. Lilian Sumner, a psychiatrist and functional medicine expert, described Wild lettuce as an herb that can improve sleep disturbed by anxiety and chronic worry, and "impart relaxation to both mind and the body"[8].

Guidance: Wild lettuce root and rhizomes are consumed medicinally as tea or tincture. Consult with a primary care doctor before use. Avoid use while pregnant or lactating. If using a commercial product, follow instructions on the package.

Wild Oats

S cientifically named Avena sativa (and commonly called "milky oats"), this grass plant is one of the most widely cultivated members of the Poaceae family. Wild oats are produced worldwide as a food crop, livestock feed, and cosmetic ingredient. It thrives in temperate regions and is recognized by its bladelike leaves, hollow stems, and the white, milky liquid it emits when squeezed (i.e., "oat milk").

Historical/Traditional Uses: Wild oats have a longstanding history of use as an aphrodisiac, anti-inflammatory, and restorative nervine. It has been used to reduce cholesterol, increase stamina, treat acne, and improve muscle function[11][16].

Psychobotanical Uses: As a mild sedative, Wild oats have been widely used to treat a host of nervous conditions, namely, anxious and depressed mood, insomnia, irritability, heart palpitations, nervous tension, fatigue due to stress, restlessness, and anxiety-related cognitive deficits[2][3][9][10][11][16]. A relatively safe plant, this herb helps people who suffer from an overstressed nervous system or anxiety-related exhaustion and weakness (that may manifest as depression)[3][8][11][16][75].

185

Widely deemed a "nerve food," it can nourish the nervous system and help achieve a sense of calm. Herbalists also tout its ability to help women manage agitation, "frazzled nerves," burn out, and exhaustion[92].

Guidance: Wild oats' green, milky tops from the immature grain are the most medicinally beneficial. They can be safely eaten (as oatmeal) or consumed as tea or tincture. For tea, add 2 tsp plant material per cup of boiling water. Drink one cup daily as needed. For tincture, add 1 part fresh plant material to 2 parts 95% alcohol (may substitute with vegetable glycerin or apple cider vinegar). Consume 1/4 tsp up to five times daily.

Wood Betony

This flowering perennial herb is a member of the Lamiaceae (Mint) family and grows native to parts of Africa, the Middle East, and Europe. Known botanically as Stachys officinalis, Wood betony is recognized by its dark green egg-shaped leaves, square stems, erect purple flower spikes, and tendency to spread in clumps. It thrives in dry open meadows, pastures, hedge banks, and woodlands. This herb commonly goes by Purple betony, Pink cotton lamb's ears, and Hedgenettels.

Historical/Traditional Uses: Wood betony has long been celebrated in ancient folklore for its spiritual uses (i.e., to ward off ghosts, evil spirits, and witchcraft). Medicinally, it was administered as an analgesic in the treatment of headaches and facial pain[11].

Psychobotanical Uses: As a mild sedative, nervine, and nerve tonic, Wood betony helps calm nervous tension, alleviate stress, achieve relaxation, calm racing thoughts, and improve sleep. It can also relieve stress-related digestive problems, reduce anxiety-related muscle tension[8], manage "frayed nerves"[11], and help "people whose minds are overactive and stressed"[9]. Shaker healers from the 19th century often celebrated this herb for its ability to treat "hysterics and nervousness"[19]. It also helps improve memory and concentration levels.

Guidance: Wood betony's dried leaves are used medicinally. For tea, add 1-2 tsp dried leaves per cup of boiled water. Cover and steep for 15-20 minutes. Drink 1 cup 2-3 times daily. For tincture, add 1 part dried leaves to 5 parts 50% alcohol (may substitute with vegetable glycerin or apple cider vinegar). Consume 1/2 tsp three times daily.

Yarrow

This invasive, perennial wildflower was once believed to conjure good luck and possess magical powers. Known as thousand-leaf, milfoil, or devil's nettle, it boasts dense clusters of small white (sometimes yellow or pink) flowers and abundant tiny leaflets. Many admire this plant's beauty and grow it as a border for ornamental gardens. Yarrow is native to Europe, Western Asia, and North America and can be found in prairies and meadows. It grows invasively and abundantly in all parts of the world and tolerates most climates. Botanically, it is known as Achillea millefolium and belongs to the Asteraceae family of sunflowers. Yarrow can be easily grown from seed.

Historical/Traditional Uses: Yarrow, a versatile herb with a longstanding history of use among Indigenous Americans, offers a wide range of traditional uses. The Cheyenne used it for cold and cough remedies, the Pawnees for pain relief, the Blackfeet as a diuretic, and the Lakota for wound healing[18]. Herbalists also applied Yarrow to aid with excessive menstrual bleeding, fevers, allergies, and problems with the circulatory, urinary, or digestive systems[3][5][6][11][16].

Its blood-staunching vulnerary properties made it the herb of choice for wound bleeding[5][6][9][15][84]. This diverse array of applications is a testament to the herb's adaptability and potential benefits.

Psychobotanical Uses: Applied to anxiety, Yarrow works as a sedative and can ease insomnia[3][5], elicit relaxation, and ameliorate anxious mood[15]. Herbalists promote this plant for its ability to induce quality sleep[96]. Previous laboratory studies have also demonstrated the significant anxiolytic effect of an orally administered extract[97].

Guidance: Yarrow's aerial parts are often used (i.e., flowers and leaves) in herbal remedies. It may be consumed in tea and tincture forms. For tea, add 1-2 tsp plant material per cup of boiling water. Drink one cup up to three times daily. For tincture, add 1 part dried plant material to 5 parts 40% alcohol (may substitute with vegetable glycerin or apple cider vinegar). Consume 1/2 tsp three times daily. People with ragweed allergies should avoid use. This plant is a known uterine stimulant, so avoid while pregnant.

Yellow Jessamine

Yellow Jessamine is a twining perennial vine with elegant trumpet-shaped yellow flowers with five rounded petals. It is also commonly called Carolina Jessamine, Carolina Jasmine, and Woodbine. Scientifically named Gelsemium sempervirens, it grows abundantly in wooded areas and thickets of Southeastern United States and Central America.

Historical/Traditional Uses: Yellow Jessamine is valued as an antispasmodic, analgesic, sedative, and central nervous system depressant. It has been used to treat neuralgia, sciatica, whooping cough, asthma, headaches, and bowel problems[11].

Psychobotanical Uses: Applied to anxiety, herbalists have administered Yellow Jessamine in the treatment of anxious mood, agitation, and insomnia[5][11]. Animal studies have also demonstrated its anxiolytic properties, namely, its ability to protect against *and* regulate anxiety[81]. More research is needed to explore the psychotherapeutic benefits of this promising plant.

Guidance: Yellow Jessamine's root is used in medicinal

preparations and consumed as root tea. For tea, add 1/2 tsp of dried root per cup of boiling water. Steep and drink 4-8 ounces daily. Consult with primary care doctor before use. The flowers can be highly toxic to humans and animals and should be handled with caution.

**The dosage recommendations listed in each chapter are general guidelines. It is important to take into consideration factors like age, weight, and general health status, as well as potential interactions with conventional medications.

Glossary

Adaptogen – An agent that helps balance, restore, and protect the body from stress, and improves the body's ability to adapt and accommodate varying stressful conditions.

Analgesic – A agent that relieve pain.

Annual – A plant that lives for one year or less and/or completes its life cycle of growing, blooming, producing seeds, and dyeing before the first frost.

Antidepressant – Substance that lessens depression.

Anxiolytic – Substance that reduces anxiety.

Biennial – A plant that completes its life cycle and lives for two seasons, usually producing only leaves the first year and flowering, fruiting, and dying in the second year.

Calmative – An agent with mild sedative and calming effects.

Cold infusion – Extraction of plant nutrients with cold water.

Concoction – A mixture or combination of various ingredients or elements.

Decoction – A method of extracting active, medicinal ingredients from a plant by boiling or simmering it in water in a covered container.

Deciduous – Plants that drop their leaves at the end of each growing season.

Elixir – The process of steeping herbs in honey or maple syrup, and combining with alcohol, glycerin, or vinegar.

Essential oil – A highly concentrated extract of the volatile components of an herb.

Evergreen – Plants that retain their leaves, never shedding all leaves at one time.

Extract – The use of a solvent to selectively remove the the the active ingredients of a plant, refining it to its most concentrated form.

Glycerite – A method of removing active, medicinal constituents of a plant by using glycerin as an extraction medium.

Herb – Plant with culinary, fragrance, cosmetic, or medicinal value.

Herbaceous – A term that applies to plants that are fleshy, with little or no woody tissues, and that tend to die back to the roots in the winter.

Hypnotic – An agent that induces sleep.

Infusion – A preparation made by soaking or steeping plant material in hot or cold water, oil (fat), alcohol, vinegar, salt, or sugar.

Native – A plant growing in its original area.

Nervine – An agent that benefits and supports the nervous system.

Neuroprotective – An agent that protects neurons from injury or degeneration and protects brain function.

Nootropic – An agent that enhances cognitive function, memory, and learning.

Glossary

Perennial – A plant that lives for two or more seasons, its green parts dying after the first frost and reappearing in the spring.

Relaxant – An agent that calms without sedating; relaxes contracted tissues.

Rhizome – A creeping, underground, horizontal stem.

Root – The portion of the plant usually found below the ground; distinguished from the stem by not having nodes.

Sedative – An agent that calms, soothes, or moderates nervousness, has a tranquilizing effect, and quiets nervous excitement.

Shrubs – Woody plants that range one to fifteen feet in height and can be deciduous or evergreen.

Strewing herb – An herb used to mask unpleasant odors.

Tea – An infusion made by simmering plant material in water.

Tincture – A concentrated medicinal preparation of plant material and alcohol, apple cider vinegar, or vegetable glycerin.

Tonic – A medicinal substance taken to restore vitality, promote vigor, and enhance well-being.

Trees – Woody plants exceeding fifteen feet in height with a vertical form; can be deciduous or evergreen.

References

(1) Crocker, P. (2018). *The herbalists' kitchen: Cooking and healing with herbs.* Sterling Epicure.

(2) Sams, T. (2020). *Herbal medicine for emotional healing: 101 natural remedies for anxiety, depression, sleep, and more.* Rockbridge Press.

(3) Balch, P. (2002). *Prescription for herbal healing: An easy-to-use A-to-Z reference to hundreds of common disorders and their herbal remedies.* Avery.

(4) University of Georgia Extension. (2021). *Georgia master gardener handbook* (8th ed.). University of Georgia.

(5) Foster, S., & Duke, J. (2014). *Peterson: Field guide to medicinal plants and herbs.* Houghton Mifflin Harcourt.

(6) Williams, K. (2021). *Dr. Sebi encyclopedia of herbs: Over 100 alkaline herbs, medicinal properties and how to use for intracellular, fully body cleanse and rejuvenation.* Alkaline Vegan Lounge.

(7) Kavanagh, J. (2017). *Medicinal herbs: A folding pocket guide to familiar widespread species.* Waterford Press.

(8). Somner, L. (2022). *Herbal medicine for mental health: Natural treatments for anxiety, depression, ADHD, and more.* Citadel Press Books.

(9). Easley, T., & Horne, S. (2016). *The modern herbal dispensatory: A medicine-making guide.* North Atlantic Books.

(10). Gladstar, R. (2012). *Rosemary Gladstar's medicinal herbs: A beginner's guide.* Storey Publishing.

(11) Chevalier, A. (2023). *Encyclopedia of herbal medicine: 560 herbs & remedies for common ailments* (4th ed.). Penguin Random House.

(12). Williams, K. (2022). *Dr. Sebi book of remedies.* Alkaline Vegan Lounge.

(13). Brown, R., Gerberg, P. & Muslin, P. (2009). *How to use herbs, nutrients, & yoga in mental health care.* W.W. Norton & Company.

(14). Boon, H., & Smith, M. (2004). *The complete natural medicine guide to the 50 most common medicinal herbs: Based on the most current scientific information from the world's leading medical journals.* Robert Rose, Inc.

(15) Castleman, M. (2009). *The new healing herbs: The essential guide to more than 130 of nature's most potent herbal remedies.* Rodale.

(16) Neal's Yard Remedies. (2020). *Essential herbs: Treat yourself naturally with herbs and homemade remedies.* DK Publishing.

References

(17) Bauer, B. (2017). *Mayo Clinic: Guide to integrative medicine: Conventional remedies meet alternative therapies to transform health*. Mayo Clinic Press.

(18). Kindscher, K. (1992). *Medicinal wild plants of the prairie: An ethnobotanical guide*. University Press of Kansas.

(19). Miller, A. (1976). *Shaker herbs: A history and a compendium*. Clarkson Potter.

(20) VanDyke, L. (2022). *African American herbalism: A practical guide to healing plants and folk traditions*. Ulysses Press.

(21). Still, C. (1998). *Botany and healing: Medicinal plants of New Jersey and the region*. Rutgers University Press.

(22) Reyes, D. (2023). *101 African American herbalism secrets: Unearthing ancient secrets for today's herbal enthusiast*. Publisher unknown.

(23) Geary, A. (2001). *The food and mood handbook: Find relief at last from depression, anxiety, PMS, cravings, and mood swings*. Thorsons.

(24). Duncan, W., & Duncan, M. (2005). *Wildflowers of the eastern United States*. University of Georgia Press.

(25) U.S. Department of Agriculture. (2024). FoodData Central. https://fdc.nal.usda.gov/fdc-app.html#/food-details/170186/nutrients

(26) Rodale Books. (2016). *Eat for extraordinary health and healing: The ultimate nutrition resource from the world's top doctors and scientists*. Rodale, Inc.

(27) Lee, M. (2014). *Working the roots: Over 400 Years of traditional African-American healing*. Wadastick Publishers.

(28) Akhondzadeh, S., Naghavi, H., Vazirian, M., Shayeganpour, A., Rashidi, H., Khani, M. Passionflower in the treatment of generalized anxiety: A pilot double-blind randomized controlled trial with Oxazepam. *Journal of Clinical Pharmacy and Therapeutics, 26*(5), 363-367.

(29) Heaton, T. (2021, August 29). Kava: The Pacific's economic diamond is being coveted by competitors. Honolulu Civil Beat. https://www.civilbeat.org/2021/08/kava-the-pacifics-economic-diamond-is-being-coveted-by-competitors/

(30) World Health Organization. (2023, September 27). Anxiety disorders. https://www.who.int/news-room/fact-sheets/detail/anxiety-disorders

(31) Cropley, M., Banks, A., & Boyle, J. (2015). The effects of rhodiola rosea L. extract on anxiety, stress, cognition and other mood symptoms. *Phytotherapy Research, 29*(12), 1934-1939.

(32) Rahbardar, M., & Hosseinzadeh, H. (2020). Therapeutic effects of rosemary (Rosmarinus officinalis L.) and its active constituents on nervous system disorders. *Iranian Journal of Basic Medical Sciences, 23*(9), 1100–1112.

(33) Voeks, R. (1997). *Sacred leaves of candomble: African magic, medicine, and religion in Brazil*. University of Texas Press.

(34) Chauhan, A., & Chauhan, V. (2020). Beneficial effects of walnuts on cognition and brain health. *Nutrients, 12*(2), 550. doi: 10.3390/nu12020550.

References

(35) Harmony, N. (2013, January 26). Harmony herbals: How to use damiana for anxiety, creativity, connection and libido. https://harmonyherbals.net/blog/how-to-use-damiana-for-natural-mental-health-herbal-highs-and-healthy-sex-drive/

(36) Poivre, M., & Duez, P. (2017). Biological activity and toxicity of the Chinese herb Magnolia officinalis Rehder & E. Wilson (Houpo) and its constituents. *Journal of Zhejiang University, 18*(3), 194–214.

(37) Talbott, S., Talbott, J., & Pugh, M. (2013). Effect of magnolia officinalis and phellodendron amurense (Relora®) on cortisol and psychological mood state in moderately stressed subjects. *Journal of the International Society of Sports Nutrition, 10*, 37.

(38) Limanaqi, F., Biagioni, F., Busceti, C., Polzella, M., Fabrizi, C., & Fornai, F. (2020). Potential antidepressant effects of scutellaria baicalensis, hericium erinaceus and rhodiola rosea. *Antioxidants, 9*(3), 234. doi: 10.3390/antiox9030234.

(39) American Psychiatric Association. (2013). *Diagnostic and statistical manual of mental disorders* (5th ed.). American Psychiatric Publishing.

(40) Mahendra, P., & Bisht, S. (2012). Ferula asafoetida: Traditional uses and pharmacological activity. *Pharmacognosy Review, 6*(12), 141–146.

(41) Sarris, J. (2024, March 2). Natural supplements for anxiety. https://www.anxiety.org/natural-anxiety-treatment-supplements

(42) Mendicino, S. (2022, April 19). Six magnolia bark benefits: Dosage & safety. https://botanicalinstitute.org/magnolia-bark/

(43) Kuphal, G. (2014). Adaptogens. https://www.va.gov/wholehealthlibrary/docs/Adaptogens.pdf.

(44) Ahmadimoghaddam, D., Sadeghian, R., Ranjbar, A., Izadidastenaei, Z., & Mohammad, S. (2020). Antinociceptive activity of Cnicus benedictus L. leaf extract: A mechanistic evaluation. *Research in Pharmaceutical Sciences, 15*(5), 463–472. doi: 10.4103/1735-5362.297849.

(45) McGrane, K. (2021, December 10). What Is Asafoetida? Benefits, side effects, and uses. https://www.healthline.com/nutrition/asafoetida-benefits

(46) Stuart, A. (2024, March 20). Muira Puama/Herbal safety. https://www.utep.edu/herbal-safety/herbal-facts/herbal%20facts%20sheet/muira-puama.html

(47) Petrides, G. (1993). *Peterson first guide to trees: The concise field guide to 243 common trees of North America.* Houghton Mifflin Company.

(48) Liu, L., Liu, C., Wang, Y., Wang, P., Li, Y., & Li, B. (2015). Herbal medicine for anxiety, depression and insomnia. *Current Neuropharmacology, 13*(4), 481–493.

(49) Mi, G., Liu, S., Zhang, J., Liang, H., Gao, Y., Li, N., Yu, B., Yang, H., & Yang, Z. (2017). Levo-tetrahydroberberrubine produces anxiolytic-like effects in mice through the 5-HT1A receptor. *PLOS ONE, 12*(1). doi: 10.1371/journal.pone.0168964.

(50) Haller, J., Krecsak, L., & Zámbori, J. (2019). Double-blind placebo controlled trial of the anxiolytic effects of a standardized Echinacea extract. *Phytotherapy Research, 34*(3), 660–668.

(51) Rabbani, M., Sajjadi, S., & Vaezi, A. (2015). Evaluation of anxiolytic and sedative effect

References

of essential oil and hydroalcoholic extract of Ocimum basilicum L. and chemical composition of its essential oil. *Research in Pharmaceutical Sciences, 10*(6), 535–543.

(52) Zhang, N., Luo, M., He, L., & Yao, L. (2020). Chemical composition of essential oil from flower of 'Shanzhizi' (gardenia jasminoides Ellis) and involvement of serotonergic system in Iis anxiolytic effect. *Molecules, 25*(20): 4702. doi: 10.3390/molecules25204702.

(53) Tao, W., Zhang, H., Xue, W., Ren, L., Xia, B., Zhou, X., Wu, H., Duan, J., & Chen, G. (2014). Optimization of supercritical fluid extraction of oil from the fruit of gardenia jasminoides and its antidepressant activity. *Molecules, 19*(12): 19350–19360.

(54) Mahomoodally, M. (2013). Traditional medicines in Africa: An appraisal of ten potent African medicinal plants. *Evidence-based Complimentary and Alternative Medicines,* 617459. doi: 10.1155/2013/617459.

(55) Walker, A., Marakis, G., Morris, A., & Robinson, P. (2002). Promising hypotensive effect of hawthorn extract: A randomized double-blind pilot study of mild, essential hypertension. *Phytotherapy Research, 16*(1), 48-54.

(56) Brendler, T., Brinckmann, J., Feiter, U., Gericke, N., Lang, L., Pozharitskaya, O., Shikov, A., Smith, M., & van Wyk, B. (2021) Sceletium for managing anxiety, depression and cognitive impairment: A traditional herbal medicine in modern-day regulatory systems. *Current Neuropharmacology, 19*(9), 1384–1400.

(57) Ritz, S. (2012, February). Plant guide for hop hornbeam (Ostrya virginiana). https://plants. usda.gov/DocumentLibrary/plantguide/pdf/pg_osvi.pdf

(58) Kroon, E., Kuhns, L., Hoch, E., & Cousijn, J. (2020). Heavy cannabis use, dependence, and the brain: A clinical perspective. *Addiction, 115*(3). 559-572.

(59) Iwu, M. (2014). *Handbook of African medicinal plants.* CRC Press.

(60) Ellingwood, F. (1919). The American materia medica, pherapeutics and Pharmacognosy. http://www.henriettesherbal.com/index.html

(61) Flausino, O.A., Zangrossi, H., Salgado, J.V., & Viana, M.B. (2002). Effects of acute and chronic treatment with Hypericum perforatum L. (LI 160) on different anxiety-related responses in rats. *Pharmacology Biochemistry and Behavior, 71*(1-2), 251–257. doi: 10.1016/s0091-3057(01)00665-7.

(62) Lehrl, S. (2004). Clinical efficacy of kava extract WS 1490 in sleep disturbances associated with anxiety disorders: Results of a multicenter, randomized, placebo-controlled, double-blind clinical trial. *Journal of Affective Disorders, 78*(2), 101-110.

(63) Pittler, M., & Ernst, E. (2003). Kava extract for treating anxiety. *The Cochrane Database of Systematic Reviews. 2003*(1). doi: 10.1002/14651858.CD003383.

(64) Singh, Y., & Singh, N. (2002). Therapeutic potential of kava in the treatment of anxiety disorders. *CNS Drugs, 16*(11), 731–743. doi: 10.2165/00023210-200216110-00002

(65) Wynn, S., & Fougère, B. (2007). Veterinary herbal medicine: A systems-based approach. *Veterinary Herbal Medicine,* 291–409. doi: 10.1016/B978-0-323-02998-8.50024-X.

(66) Bhattacharya, S.K., Bhattacharya, A., Sairam, K., & Ghosal, S. Anxiolytic-antidepressant activity of Withania somnifera glycowithanolides: An experimental study. *Phytomedicine, 7.* 463–469.

References

(67) Louis, M., & Kowalski, S.D. (2002). Use of aromatherapy with hospice patients to decrease pain, anxiety, and depression and to promote an increased sense of well-being. *American Journal Hospital Palliative Care, 19*(6), 381-386.

(68) Dimond, C., Dovan, K., Shah, S., Tran, B., Pham, K., Hsu, K., Nguyen, N., & O'Dell, K. (2023). Effect of Nelumbo nucifera extract on anxiety symptoms in individuals with moderate to severe anxiety: An exploratory study. *Journal of Contemporary Pharmacy Practice, 70*(2a), 15–20.

(69) Sugimoto, Y., Furutani, S., Itoh, A., Tanahashi, T., Nakajima, H., Oshiro, H., Sun, S., & Yamada, J. (2008). Effects of extracts and neferine from the embryo of Nelumbo nucifera seeds on the central nervous system. *Phytomedicine, 15*(12), 1117-1124. doi: 10.1016/j.phymed.2008.09.005.

(70) Kulkarni, M., & Juvekar, A. (2009). Anti-anxiety effects of leaves of Nelumbo nucifera gaertn in mice. *Pharmacologyonline,* 2. 292– 299.

(71) Ekiert, H., Pajor, J., Klin, P., Rzepiela, A., Ślesak, H., & Szopa, A. (2020). Significance of Artemisia Vulgaris L. (common mugwort) in the history of medicine and its possible contemporary applications substantiated by phytochemical and pharmacological studies. *Molecules, 25*(19), 4415. doi: 10.3390/molecules25194415.

(72) Anibogwu, R., De Jesus, K., Pradhan, S., Pashikanti, S., Mateen, S., & Sharma, K. (2021). Extraction, isolation and characterization of bioactive compounds from Artemisia and their biological significance: A review. *Molecules, 16*(22), 6995. doi: 10.3390/molecules26226995.

(73) Manganyi, M., Bezuidenhout, C., Regnier, T., & Ateba, C. (2021). A chewable cure "Kanna": Biological and pharmaceutical properties of Sceletium tortuosum. *Molecules, 26*(9): doi: 10.3390/molecules26092557.

(74) Reay, J., Wetherall, M., Norton, E., Lillis, J., & Badmaev. V. (2020). Sceletium tortuosum (Zembrin®) ameliorates experimentally induced anxiety in healthy volunteers. *Human Psychopharmacology: Clinical and Experimental. 35*(6), 1-7.

(75) Stansbury, J. (2020). *Herbal formularies for health professionals, Vol. 4: Neurology, psychiatry, and pain management: Including cognitive and neurologic conditions and emotional conditions.* Chelsea Green Publishing.

(76) Caro, D., Rivera, D., Ocampo, Y., Franco, L., & Salas, R. (2018). Pharmacological evaluation of mentha spicata L. and plantago major L., medicinal plants used to treat anxiety and insomnia in Colombian Caribbean coast. *Evidence-based Complementary and Alternative Medicine,* 5921514. doi: 10.1155/2018/5921514

(77) Ilgün, S., Akkol, E., Ilhan, M., Polat, D., Coşkun, A., & Sobarzo-Sánchez, E. (2020). Sedative effects of latexes obtained from some lactuca L. species growing in Turkey. *Molecules, 25*(7), 1587. https://doi.org/10.3390/molecules25071587.

(78) Pan, W., Shi, H., Zang, Z., Meng, Q., Cheng, Y., Liang, L., Zhai, Y., Yin, G., Sun, L., & Ma, K. (2024). Research progress on classical traditional Chinese medicine formula Baihe Zhimu (Lilium lancifolium bulb and Anemarrhena asphodeloides rhizome) decoction in the treatment of depression. *Heliyon, 10*(3). doi: 10.1016/j.heliyon.2024.e25171.

References

(79) Alonso-Castro, A., Domínguez, F., Ruiz-Padilla, A., Campos-Xolalpa, N., Zapata-Morales, J., Carranza-Alvarez, C., & Maldonado-Miranda, J. (2017). Medicinal plants from North and Central America and the Caribbean considered toxic for humans: The other side of the coin. *Evidence Based Complementary Alternative Medicine, 2.* 1-28. doi: 10.1155/2017/9439868.

(80) Ibarra-Alvarado, C., Rojas, A., Mendoza, S., Bah, M., Gutierrez, D.M., Hernandez-Sandoval, L., & Martinez, M.(2010). Vasoactive and antioxidant activities of plants used in Mexican traditional medicine for the treatment of cardiovascular diseases. *Pharmaceutical Biology, 48*(7). 732-739. doi: 10.3109/13880200903271280.

(81) Long, J., Tang, M., Zuo, M., Xu, W., Meng, S., & Liu, Z. (2023). The antianxiety effects of koumine and gelsemine, two main active components in the traditional Chinese herbal medicine Gelsemium: A comprehensive review. *Brain-X, 1*(4).

(82) Mitchell, F. (1999). *Hoodoo medicine: Gullah herbal remedies.* Summerhouse Press.

(83) Brock, C., Whitehouse, J., Tewfik, I., & Towell, T. (2010). American skullcap (Scutellaria lateriflora): An ancient remedy for today's anxiety? *British Journal of Wellbeing, 1*(4). 25-30.

(84) Felter, H., & Lloyd, J. (1905). *King's American dispensatory*, Vol. 1 of 2 (19th ed.). The Ohio Valley Company.

(85) Wolfson, P. & Hoffmann, D.L. (2003). An investigation into the efficacy of Scutellaria lateriflora in healthy volunteers. *Alternative Therapies in Health and Medicine, 9.* 74-78.

(86) Saeed, S., Bloch, R., & Antonacci, D. (2007). Herbal and dietary supplements for treatment of anxiety disorders. *American Family Physician, 76*(4), 549-556. https://www.aafp.org/pubs/afp/issues/2007/0815/p549.html

(87) Blumenthal, M. (2003). *The ABC clinical guide to herbs.* American Botanical Council.

(88) Lee, S., Shin, Y., Lee, J., & Seol, G. (2023). Inhalation of Origanum majorana L. essential oil while working reduces perceived stress and anxiety levels of nurses in a COVID-19 intensive care unit: A randomized controlled trial. *Frontiers in Psychiatry, 17.* doi: 10.3389/fpsyt.2023.1287282.

(89) The Complete German Commission E Monograph. (1999). Therapeutic guide to herbal medicines. https://www.herbalgram.org/resources/commission-e-monographs/monograph-unapproved-herbs/mugwort/

(90) Spinella, M. (2001). *The psychopharmacology of herbal medicine: Plant drugs that alter mind, brain, and behavior.* The MIT Press.

(91) Drugs.com. (2024). Lobelia. https://www.drugs.com/npp/lobelia.html.

(92) Silverstein, S., & Golant, S. (2018). *Moodtopia: Tame your moods, de-stress, and find balance using herbal remedies, aromatherapy, and more.* Da Copa Press.

(93) Bisong, S., Brown, R., & Osim, E. (2010). Comparative effects of Rauwolfia vomitoria and chlorpromazine on locomotor behaviour and anxiety in mice. *Journal of Ethnopharmacology, 132*(1). 334-339.

(94) Jin, Z., Gao, N., Zhang, J., , Li, X., Chen, H., Xiong, J., Li, Y., & Tang, Y. (2014). The discovery of Yuanzhi-1, a triterpenoid saponin derived from the traditional Chinese medi-

References

cine, has antidepressant-like activity. *Progress in Neuro-Psychopharmacology & Biological Psychiatry, 53*(4). 9-14.

(95) Apeokarang, N. (2024). A Haitian Treasure: Vèvenn (Vervain). https://www.drnaika.com/blog/a-haitian-treasure-vvenn-vervain.

(96) E. Mindell. (2022). *Dr. Earl Mindell's herb bible: Fight depression and anxiety, improve your sex life, prevent illness, and heal faster – the all natural way.* Atria Paperback.

(97) Baretta, I., Felizardo, R., Bimbato, V., dos Santos, M., Kassuya, C., Gasparotto Junior, A., da Silva, C., de Oliveira, S., Ferreira, J., & Andreatini, R. (2012). Anxiolytic-like effects of acute and chronic treatment with Achillea millefolium L. extract. *Journal of Ethnopharmacology, 140*(1). 46-54.

(98) Fajemiroye, J., Adam, K., Jordan, Z., Alves, C., & Aderoju, A. (2018) Evaluation of anxiolytic and antidepressant-like activity of aqueous leaf extract of Nymphaea lotus linn. in mice. *Journal of Iranian Pharmaceutical Research, 17*(2), 613-626.

(99) Bhattacharyya, D., Sur, T., Jana, U., & Debnath, P. (2008). Controlled programmed trial of Ocimum sanctum leaf on generalized anxiety disorders. *Nepal Medical College Journal, 10*(3). 176-179.

(100) Chen, W., He, R., Li, Y., Li, S., Tsoi, B., & Kurihara, H. (2011). Pharmacological studies on the anxiolytic effect of standardized Schisandra lignans extract on restraint-stressed mice. *Phytomedicine, 18*(13). 1144-1147.

(101) Gladstar, R. (1999). *Herbs for stress and anxiety: How to make and use herbal remedies to strengthen the nervous system.* Storey Publishing.

(102) Patel, S., Ray, R., Sharma, A., Mehta, V., Katyal, A., & Udayabanu, M. (2018). Antidepressant and anxiolytic like effects of Urtica dioica leaves in streptozotocin induced diabetic mice. *Metabolic Brain Disease, 33*(4). 1281-1292.

(103) Covey, H. (2007). African American slave medicine: Herbal and non-herbal treatments. Lexington Books.

Photo Credits

American ginseng - Weber, 2021

American ginseng root – USGS Bee Inv. & Mon. Lab, Beltsville, MD, 2018

Asafoetida - Spline_x, 2023

Assafoetida (Ferula plant) - Valery Fassiaux, 2012 *

Ashwagandha - Sadasiba Behera, 2023

Bacopa - Selko H, 2024

Baikal skullcap - AntaresNS, 2023

Basil - Robyn Mac, 2015

Basil – David J. Stang, 2006 *

Black cohosh - Skymoon13, 2018

Black haw - Skymoon13, 2018

Black walnut - P.A. Collins, 2019

Blessed thistle - Emer1940, 2022

Blessed thistle – Wikipedia, 2009 *

Blue vervain - Ana Lebiodiene, 2022

California poppy - Voren1, 2020

California poppy – Joyce Cory, 2020

Cannabis - Alexandrum79, 2019

Cannabis sativa – Gilles Ayotte, Bibliothèque de l'Université Laval, 2023*

Catnip - miwa_in_oz, 2016

Chamomile - Valentyn Volkov, 2016

Chamomile - Zana Strkovska, 2017

Chinese polygala - J.M.Garg, 2008

Codonopsis root - chengyuzheng, 2023

Codonopsis – Stanislav Doronenko, 2007 *

Corydalis - Multik7, 2015

Cucumber magnolia - Kristine Radkovska, 2023

Cucumber tree - James St. John, 2008 *

Cramp bark - Angeline Teixeira, 2021

Damiana - Eskymaks, 2018

Damiana – Katherine Wagner-Reiss, 2018 *

Dropwort - cowii, 2021

Echinacea - Sergey and Marina, 2022

Echinacea - FreCha, 2023

Egyptian blue lotus - Ermell, 2009

Photo Credits

Eleuthero - Goroda, 2019

European bugleweed - Spline_x, 2018

European bugleweed – Gilles Ayotte, Biblio. de l'Université Laval, 2023 *

Figwort - Ian Redding, 2016

Gardenia – John Robert McPherson, 2010 *

Gardenia - Juicybits, 2011

Gardenia - Juicybits, 2011

Ginkgo - Bonchan, 2015

Gotu kola - Unkwn, 2019

Hawthorn - Scisettialfio, 2020

Hawthorn – Stefan Lefnaer, 2018 *

Holy basil - PosiNote, 2019

Hop hornbeam - Erika Mitchell, 2013

Hops - NetPix, 2023

Indian pipe - Yves Dery, 2020

Indian tobacco - Safeer Ahmed, 2018

Jamaican dogwood - Francisco Herrera, 2023

Kava ceremony in Fiji - Powerofforever - 2022

Kava leaves - chameleonseye, 2017

Lavender - nito100, 2012

Lavender fields – Unknown, 2012

Lemon balm - Scisettialfio, 2017

Lemon verbena - PicturePartners, 2012

Linden - Plant Image Library, 2016

Magnolia - Togmit, 2007

Matrimony Vine – Lazare Gagnidze, 2012 *

Mimosa - Scisettialfio, 2020

Mimosa - Andrey Butko, 2006 *

Motherwort - al_ter, 2020

Mugwort - R.A. Nonemacher, 2018 *

Muira puama - Arif Vector, 2022

Muira Puama - Armando G. Stuart (Univ. Tx-El Paso)

Northern prickly ash - Marina Denisenko, 2022

Passionflower - Yummy pic, 2022

Peppermint - Yasonya, 2019

Pink lady's slippers - wbritten, 2011

Poison devil's pepper – JJi-Elle , 2018

Pulsatilla - Cristi Croitoru, 2021

Rhodiola - Inventori, 2022

Rosemary - klenova, 2013

Sacred Lotus – T. Voekler, 2008

Photo Credits

Sceletium – Krzysztof Ziarnek, Kenraiz, 2022

Schisandra chinensis - spline_x, 2019

Skullcap - skymoon13, 2019

Skunk cabbage - Robert Winkler, 2019

Spearmint - LFO62, 2020

St. John's wort - Scisettialfio, 2017

Stinging nettle – Uwe H. Friese, 2003 *

Sweet everlasting - Brian Woolman, 2023

Sweet marjoram – Carlo Brescia, 2022 *

Tall blue lettuce – Gilles Ayotte, Bibliothèque de l'Univ. Laval, 1948*

Thyme - Scisettialfio, 2017

Tiger lily - Ana-Maria Oprisoreanu, 2018

Twinleaf - Krzysztof Ziarnek, Kenraiz, 2019

Valerian - Milena Katzer, 2018

Viper's bugloss - Danut Vieru, 2023

Viper's bugloss – Peter O'Connor, 2012 *

Virgin's bower - Nick Kurzenko, 2017

Wild cherry - aga7ta, 2021

Wild ginger - Kay Dropiewski, 2022

Wild lettuce - Hamid Photography, 2023

Wild oats - H. Zell, 2009 *

Wood betony - Wirestock, 2022

Yarrow - Orzeczenie, 2008

Yellow jessamine - Stacy Matte, 2022

Yellow lady's slippers - Doug Gordon, 2019

*Sourced for Wikimedia Commons

Index

207

Index

Index

Index

Index

Index

Index

Index

Index

Index

About the Author

Dr. Lydia Odenat is a licensed psychologist, author, and educator specializing in trauma-informed care and power-based psychology. She promotes a holistic approach to psychotherapy that focuses on the mind-body-spirit-nature continuum. Dr. Odenat founded the Georgia Psychological Treatment Center (GPTC), a multi-specialty group practice in Marietta, GA.